ROCKS AND MINERALS

ROC

MINERALS

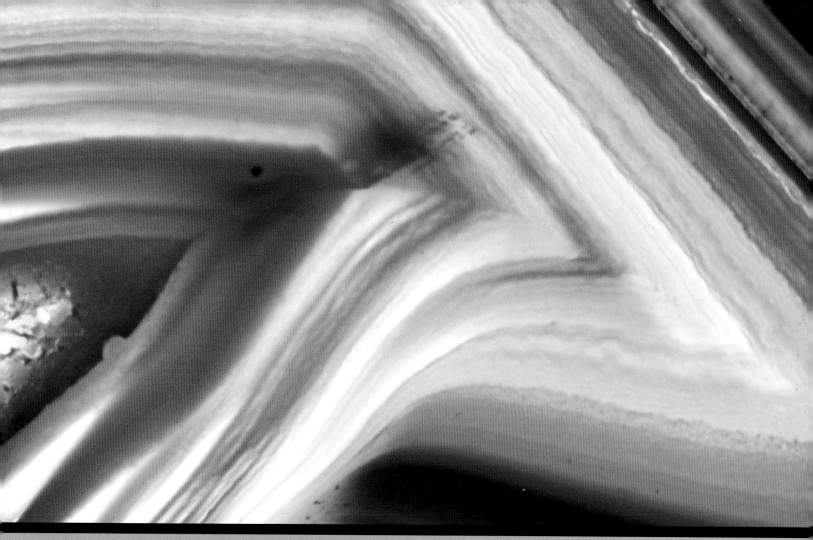

SLICE OF AGATE

CKS AND

DAN GREEN

SCHOLASTIC discover more™

Rock Collector *digital book*

Download your free digital book and become an expert rock hound! Rock Collector is packed with information about finding and identifying a treasure trove of rocks and minerals. There are lots of great pictures to help you.

Your digital book is very simple to use. Enter the code (bottom right) to download it to any Mac or PC. Open it in Adobe Reader, also free to download. Then you're all set!

ROCK COLLECTO

A digital companion to Rocks and Min

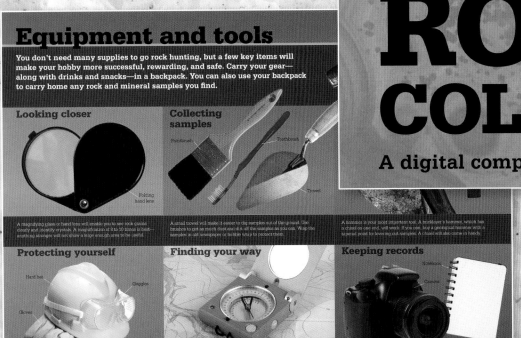

Equipment and tools

You don't need many supplies to go rock hunting, but a few key items will make your hobby more successful, rewarding, and safe. Carry your gear— along with drinks and snacks—in a backpack. You can also use your backpack to carry home any rock and mineral samples you find.

Looking closer

Folding hand lens

A magnifying glass or hand lens will enable you to see rock grains clearly and identify crystals. A magnification of 8 to 10 times is best— anything stronger will not show a large enough area to be useful.

Collecting samples

Paintbrush

Toothbrush

Trowel

A small trowel will make it easier to dig samples out of the ground. Use brushes to get as much dust and dirt off the samples as you can. Wrap the samples in old newspaper or bubble wrap to protect them.

A hammer is your most important tool. A bricklayer's hammer, which has a chisel on one end, will work. If you can, buy a geological hammer with a tapered point for levering out samples. A chisel will also come in handy.

Protecting yourself

Hard hat

Goggles

Gloves

Striking a rock with a hammer may send splinters flying, so always wear goggles to protect your eyes. Also essential are strong gloves to protect your hands and a hard hat to guard against falling rocks.

Finding your way

You will need a compass and a topographical map (one that shows contour lines) to navigate. Try to get a geological map (like the one above), too. Its color coding will show you which rocks you're likely to find, and where.

Keeping records

Notebook

Camera

Record where and when you make your finds in a notebook. Label your samples immediately, using pens and stickers. If you have a camera, or a phone with one, photograph the site and any specimens that you can't dig out.

Hyperlinks

All the pages in the digital book are hyperlinked. Click the colored buttons for more facts and pictures, video clips, and tips for using your digital book.

All you need

Every rock hound needs to be properly equipped. Your digital book is full of tips about the best tools, equipment, and clothing. Data files give you essential information about hundreds of rocks, and there are in-depth profiles of common and especially interesting ones.

" Mineral substances vary greatly in color, transparency, luster, brilliance, odor, taste, . . . shape, and form. "

—GEORGIUS AGRICOLA, 1546

Granite [Last rock standing!]

Supertough granite is the most common of all the intrusive igneous rocks—those that form underground from magma. It takes a lot to break granite down, so granite survives long after the softer rock around it has been weathered away. Because it is so durable, granite is often used as a building material and for making monuments. At Mount Rushmore, in South Dakota, the huge faces of four US presidents have been carved into the granite cliffs.

Yosemite's Half Dome probably formed around
87 million
years ago

📹 See Mount Rushmore up close

📷 Extrusive rocks gallery

Half Dome, Yosemite, CA
Granite forms deep below the surface in dome-shaped masses called batholiths. Half Dome is part of a batholith, uplifted by **mountain building** and exposed by weathering.

Mineral makeup
The exact mineral composition of the different types of granite varies, but all granites contain feldspar, quartz, and mica. Feldspar is the dominant mineral.

White granite
White alkali feldspar
Gray quartz
Black biotite mica

Data file: granite
Speckly granite often has coarse (large) grains. It forms from slow-cooling magma, so the crystal grains have a long time to grow. Granite makes mountain peaks, rocky outcrops, and the **tors** of moorland areas. It forms boulders and fragments in valleys carved out by **glaciers**.

What it is	Intrusive igneous rock
Color	White, gray, pink, or red
Major minerals	Feldspar, quartz, mica
Texture	Medium- to coarse-grained

Pink granite

Granite building
Durable granite is often used to face prestigious buildings, like the Utah State Capitol in Salt Lake City. Beautiful when sliced and polished, it also makes impressive coverings for interior floors and walls.

🔍 **discover more**—other intrusive rocks

💎 How to be a rock hunter

Mount Rushmore

From high up on the cliffs of Mount Rushmore, the 60-foot-tall (18 m) heads of four US presidents—George Washington, Thomas Jefferson, Theodore Roosevelt, and Abraham Lincoln—stare out majestically across the South Dakota landscape. The mountain's granite rock is ideal for a memorial intended to last for a long time, since it erodes at a rate of just 1 inch (25 mm) every 10,000 years.

Work on these awesome sculptures, which were designed by the Danish-American artist Gutzon Borglum, began in 1927. It was a dangerous project. Most of the granite was blasted away with dynamite. Then the facial features were shaped using drills and chisels. As they worked, the carvers sat in swinging seats called "bosun's chairs" that were suspended by cables from the top of the 500-foot (150 m) cliffs.

The sculptures that form the Mount Rushmore National Memorial are located along the northeastern edge of the Harney Peak Granite Batholith, in South Dakota's Black Hills. This batholith formed when rising magma entered older "host" schist rocks and began to cool, around 1.7 billion years ago. The granite became exposed about 50 million years ago, and since then weathering has shaped the Black Hills into their present form.

It took
14 years
to carve Mount Rushmore out of granite

A cone of rock debris called scree lies under the sculptures. Scree can be formed by weathering, but here it is made up of fragments from the carving process.

In-depth info
To discover even more, click the colored words to link to encyclopedia pages with in-depth articles on essential topics. Glossary entries explain difficult terms.

ENTER

📚 **SCHOLASTIC** discover more

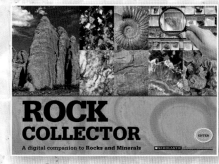

Consultant: Dr. Antony Burnham, Bristol University, UK

Literacy Consultant: Barbara Russ, 21st Century Community Learning Center Director for Winooski (Vermont) School District

Project Editors: Tom Jackson, Steve Setford

Project Art Editor: Mark Lloyd

Art Director: Bryn Walls

US Editor: Esther Lin

Managing Editor: Miranda Smith

Managing Production Editor: Stephanie Engel

Cover Designer: Neal Cobourne

DTP: John Goldsmid

Digital Photography Editor: Stephen Chin

Visual Content Project Manager: Diane Allford-Trotman

Executive Director of Photography, Scholastic: Steve Diamond

> **"Rocks are the record of events that took place at the time they formed. They are books. They have a different vocabulary, a different alphabet, but you learn how to read them."**
> —JOHN MCPHEE, JOURNALIST AND WRITER

Library of Congress Cataloging-in-Publication Data Available

ISBN 978-0-545-50511-6

10 9 8 7 6 5 4 3 2 1   13 14 15 16 17

Printed in Singapore   46
First edition, September 2013

Scholastic is constantly working to lessen the environmental impact of our manufacturing processes. To view our industry-leading paper procurement policy, visit www.scholastic.com/paperpolicy.

EXPLOSIVES CRACKING OPEN ROCKY GROUND

Contents

New rock factory

Rivers of red-hot lava flow down the sides of Ecuador's Tungurahua volcano. Tungurahua, which means "throat of fire" in the native Quechua language, erupts every 100 years or so. Fluid molten rock, called magma, rises from deep under this fiery mountain and explodes from the summit, then cools and hardens to form new rock. Tiny particles of rocks, minerals, and volcanic glass are hurled more than a mile high in a gray cloud of ash that can cause chaos for local people.

Mineral riches

In this overhead view of a sulfur mine in Senegal, Africa, a huge mountain of bright yellow sulfur crystals makes dump trucks look like toys. The mineral sulfur is used in fertilizers, which help crops grow, and it is added to rubber tires to toughen them. It is also what makes match heads catch fire. Many of the world's raw materials, including sulfur, are buried underground. We dig out billions of tons of rocks and minerals from huge mines every year.

Inside Ear

* How do crystals grow inside rocks?

* How deep a hole can you drill into Earth?

* How many stone blocks are there in the Great Pyramid?

Meet the planet! [Rock

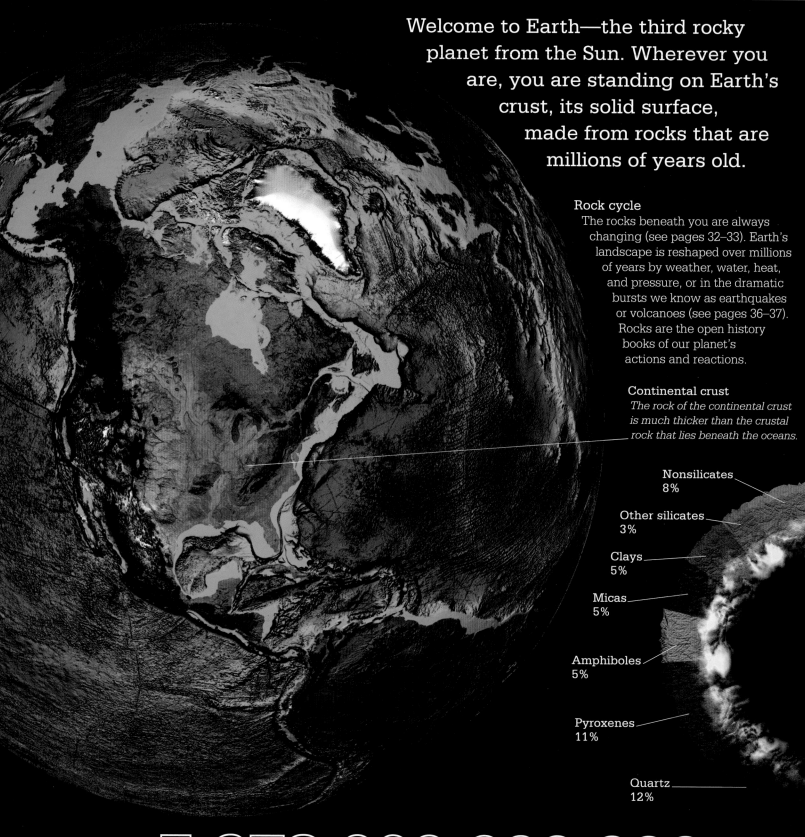

Welcome to Earth—the third rocky planet from the Sun. Wherever you are, you are standing on Earth's crust, its solid surface, made from rocks that are millions of years old.

Rock cycle

The rocks beneath you are always changing (see pages 32–33). Earth's landscape is reshaped over millions of years by weather, water, heat, and pressure, or in the dramatic bursts we know as earthquakes or volcanoes (see pages 36–37). Rocks are the open history books of our planet's actions and reactions.

Continental crust

The rock of the continental crust is much thicker than the crustal rock that lies beneath the oceans.

Nonsilicates
8%

Other silicates
3%

Clays
5%

Micas
5%

Amphiboles
5%

Pyroxenes
11%

Quartz
12%

Earth is a 5,972,000,000,000,

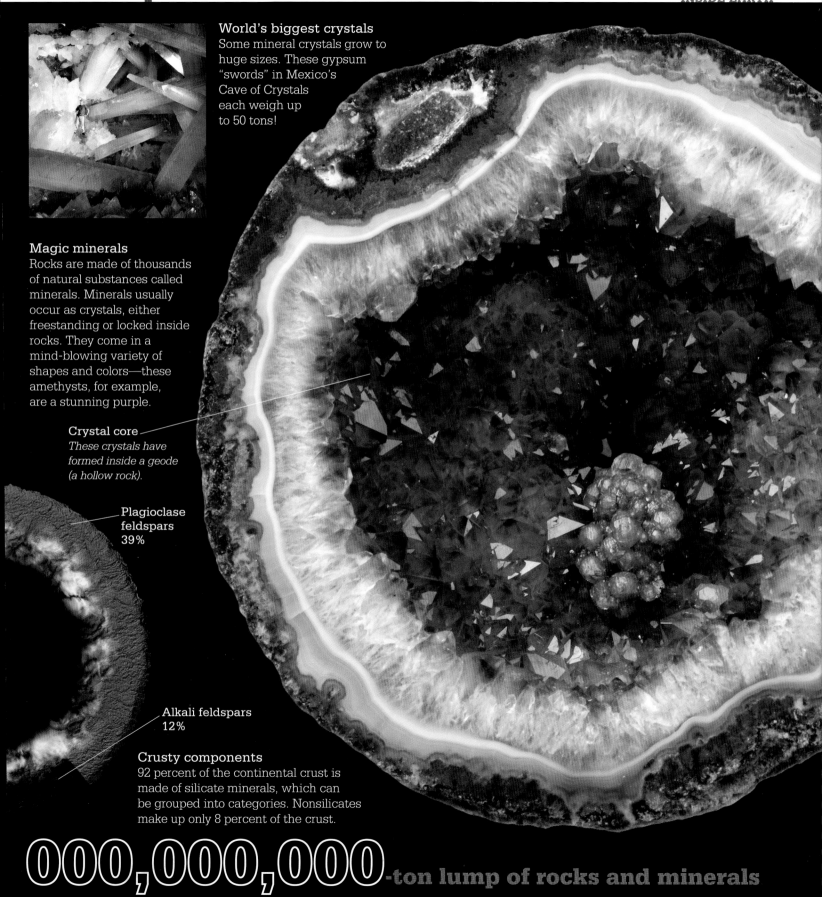

World's biggest crystals

Some mineral crystals grow to huge sizes. These gypsum "swords" in Mexico's Cave of Crystals each weigh up to 50 tons!

Magic minerals

Rocks are made of thousands of natural substances called minerals. Minerals usually occur as crystals, either freestanding or locked inside rocks. They come in a mind-blowing variety of shapes and colors—these amethysts, for example, are a stunning purple.

Crystal core

These crystals have formed inside a geode (a hollow rock).

Plagioclase feldspars 39%

Alkali feldspars 12%

Crusty components

92 percent of the continental crust is made of silicate minerals, which can be grouped into categories. Nonsilicates make up only 8 percent of the crust.

000,000,000-ton lump of rocks and minerals

Minerals vs. rocks

Cut open a rock, and you'll see that it is made of many different minerals. Cut open a mineral, and it's the same all the way through. That's because a given mineral is made of repeating blocks of atoms.

Chemical combinations

A mineral may be made of a single chemical element, but usually a mineral is a compound—a combination of more than one element. The atoms in the elements combine together in a repeated, orderly pattern to form the specific crystal structure of that mineral.

Orpiment crystal

Brown beauty
These long yellow-brown crystals are orpiment, a compound containing the elements sulfur and arsenic.

Close-up clues

Geologists—scientists who study Earth's history through its rocks—can identify a rock from the kinds of minerals it contains. If you think that diorite looks dull, put this salt-and-pepper rock under a microscope to reveal the tiny, beautiful crystals composing it!

DIORITE

Diorite enlarged
This extraordinary rainbow of colors is produced by shining a beam of light through a slice of rock. Geologists have to cut the rock into ultrathin slices—this slice is five times thinner than a postage stamp, thin enough to make it transparent.

Magnification
This plagioclase crystal is about 0.08 inches (2 mm) across.

collections]

Understanding rocks

Geologists organize rocks based on how they were formed. They divide them into three main types: igneous, sedimentary, and metamorphic.

BASALT

Igneous rocks

This type of rock forms when a molten material called magma cools and solidifies. Some igneous rocks form under the ground. Others, like basalt, are made when magma erupts from volcanoes as lava.

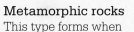
SANDSTONE

Sedimentary rocks

These rocks are made from grains and particles that settle on the ground and form deposits called sediments. Layers build up over years, until they are pressed into solid rock. Sandstone is made from thick layers of sand.

GNEISS

Metamorphic rocks

This type forms when older rocks are squeezed and heated by huge forces inside Earth, such as those that push up mountains. This gneiss shows the ripples caused by the immense pressure.

Earth has about

3,000

types of minerals

HAWAI'I VOLCANOES NATIONAL PARK, HI

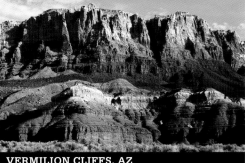
VERMILION CLIFFS, AZ

TATRA MOUNTAINS, POLAND

More here

For key to symbols, see page 112.

thunder egg quartz
Keokuk geodes
James Hutton gneiss
igneous **sedimentary metamorphic**

National Geographic Kids: Everything Rocks and Minerals
by Steve Tomecek

Backpack Books: 1001 Facts About Rocks and Minerals
by Sue Fuller and Chris Maynard

Visit **Crystal Cave** in Put-in-Bay, OH, to see the world's largest geode.

Geode State Park, in Iowa, displays a collection of geodes found in the park.

geologist: a scientist who specializes in the study of the origin, history, and structure of Earth.

solidify: to change from a liquid to a solid form.

Crystal bubbles

Although they look like regular dull-colored rocks on the outside, geodes have hollow centers lined with glittering minerals. These natural wonders form when large crystals (often quartz) grow in empty spaces inside of rocks.

MAKING A GEODE

1 Bubble trap
Gas bubbles in hot magma get stuck as it solidifies, leaving empty space.

2 Slow drip
Mineral-rich waters trickle through, gradually depositing minerals.

3 Crystal crust
The space fills with crystals.

Bright rainbow colors make tourmaline (center and far right) one of the most colorful minerals on Earth. The pink version was collected by the last empress of China, Cixi (1835–1908), who bought large amounts of the gem from the Himalaya Mine in California. And this is just one of many extraordinary rocks and minerals.

OPAL

COPPER

EMERALD

SMITHSONITE

PENTAGONITE

KYANITE

SANDSTONE

PYROMORPHITE

LABRADORITE

SCHIST

CHALCEDONY

GALENA (SPHERES)

HALITE
(ROCK SALT)

HEULANDITE

ARAGONITE

CUPRO-
AUSTINITE

FLUORITE

DIOPTASE

SULFUR

ORPIMENT

WULFENITE

GYROLITE

AMBER

CALCITE

TOURMALINE

ADAMITE

GARNET

THOMSONITE

WAVELLITE

TOURMALINE

COBALTOAN
DOLOMITE

MOLYBDENITE

BARITE

OBSIDIAN

PYRITE

LIMESTONE

RHODOCHROSITE

How to make a planet

The history of rocks and minerals is the history of our planet. Billions of years ago, their raw materials were specks in a spinning disk of dust. They combined to make a ball with a hot mineral core and a thin outer layer of solid rock—planet Earth.

1.5% Calcium
This is a metal found in animal shells and bones.

1.4% Aluminum
This is the most common metal element in Earth's crust.

1.1% Other elements
This includes everything from antimony to zinc. The rarest element is francium. All of Earth's rocks together contain just 1 ounce (28 g) of francium.

32% Iron
Iron is made inside Sun-size stars right before they die.

SUN

30% Oxygen
This gas makes up 20 percent of the air and is the most common element in minerals.

Elements inside Earth

The minerals that combined to form our planet are made of one or more elements. There are 92 elements that occur in Earth, but almost all of the planet's minerals are made up of just 8 of them.

40,230 ft.
(12,262 m): the deepest hole ever drilled into Earth's crust

Recipe for planet Earth

How can you make a planet that's hard on the outside but soft in the middle? You'll need a thin crust that covers a doughy interior and a hot, gooey core with a solid center.

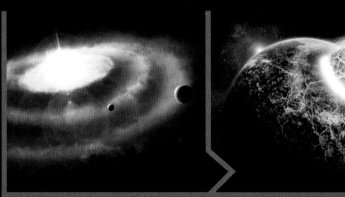

1 Start with a dust cloud
Take a cloud of gas and dust and spin it around a fresh star, like the Sun. Mineral flecks will join together, and the planet will grow as gravity pulls in more material.

2 Mix it up
There will now be a few large, rocky lumps. Smash them together. The collisions will melt them into a single molten mass.

2%

Nickel
Miners often confused this metal with the more valuable copper, so they named it for "Old Nick," the devil!

3%

Sulfur
This is one of the few elements that occurs in pure form on Earth, often around volcanoes.

14%

Magnesium
This metal is commonly found dissolved in seawater.

15%

Silicon
This element is found in sand and is used in glass, concrete, and computer chips.

Earth in layers

Underneath the rocks of Earth's crust is the mantle. The uppermost part is rigid rock that gradually turns into mushy magma. Earth's center is a liquid core with a solid heart of the minerals iron and nickel.

Crust
This is only 4.5 miles (7 km) thick under the oceans, but it is 10 times as thick on land.

Upper mantle
This is made of soft rock, which melts into the magma that erupts from volcanoes as lava.

Lower mantle
About 410–1,860 miles (660–2,990 km) down, this layer is half melted into gooey magma.

Outer core
This is a blob of liquid iron and nickel 1,860–3,200 miles (2,990–5,150 km) beneath our feet.

Inner core
Great pressure makes the metals solid. It is almost as hot down here as it is on the Sun's surface.

Atmosphere
Light gases form the sky; there are no minerals here.

CRUST

LOWER MANTLE

OUTER CORE

INNER CORE

3 Squeeze the planet
Gravity will help now, squashing the planet into a tighter ball. This will release more energy and keep the surface bubbling. Meteor strikes will turn up the heat.

4 Slowly bake
The planet's layers will form at temperatures above 2,820°F (1,550°C). Dense minerals, such as metals, will sink to the center, while lighter minerals will float to the surface.

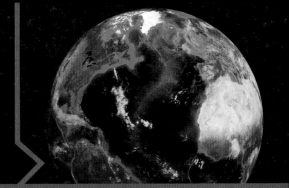

5 Create a perfect crust
As the surface cools, the lighter minerals will form a crunchy crust. The rocks will sweat out a steamy atmosphere and liquid oceans. Allow to stand for 4.6 billion years.

Made of stone [Built

Humans have used the rocks of Earth's crust for millennia, for shelter and for their most impressive buildings. Of the original Seven Wonders of the Ancient World, only the pyramids of Egypt remain intact today. The giant blocks of stone that form the base of the Great Pyramid, still the largest stone building on Earth, cover an amazing 13.6 acres (5.5 hectares).

Stone Age tools
This flint cutter is 1.6 million years old. It was sharpened by prehistoric peoples to cut up meat or plants.

Cutting with water
The ancient Egyptians were expert masons, or stoneworkers. They did not need tough drills or rock saws. Instead, they cut blocks of stone with wet wooden wedges. They used dolerite hammerstones to shape the stone.

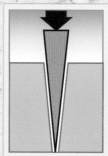  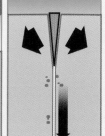

1 Hammer A wedge of wood was hammered into a crack in a rock.

2 Soak Water was poured onto the wedge and left to soak in.

3 Split The wet wood swelled sideways and split the stone.

Ages of stone
Over the last 6,000 years, stone has been chosen for some of the world's most impressive buildings because it resists weathering and aging. Humans have learned how to cut it into shapes and to use gluelike cement to seal blocks together. Today's largest buildings contain concrete, an artificial stone.

Simple slabs
The earliest stone monuments are made from megaliths ("big stones"). These are huge, flat slabs, cut whole from mountainsides.

POULNABRONE DOLMEN, IRELAND

CA. **2900** BCE

Cut to fit
The Great Pyramid has 2 million limestone blocks, each one cut to an exact shape. It was the world's tallest building until 1311 CE, when England's Lincoln Cathedral claimed the title.

GREAT PYRAMID OF GIZA, EGYPT

CA. **2540** BCE

Block work
Most of the Great Wall of China is made from bricks cemented into a mighty barrier designed to keep invaders out. The brick building blocks were made from mud that hardened when heated.

GREAT WALL OF CHINA

1570 CE

Liquid stone

Concrete is sand and clay stuck together by quicklime cement, which is made by burning limestone. Water is then added to make a thick liquid that can be poured into any shape. When dry, it sets as hard as stone. It is used in everything from skyscrapers to sidewalks.

Make an impression
Celebrities leave their hand- and footprints in wet concrete on the Hollywood Walk of Fame.

150 billion: the number of grains in 1 lb. (450 g) of concrete

Concrete core
Skyscrapers are supported by steel girders—but stone is still needed to hold them up. The girders jut out from thick concrete pillars deep inside the buildings.

SHANGHAI WORLD FINANCIAL CENTER, CHINA

2008

Smooth surface
Most of the Taj Mahal, a majestic monument to an Indian queen, is built from inexpensive bricks. But the shimmering exterior is made of polished marble.

Big barrier
The wall runs 5,500 miles (8,850 km) through northern China.

TAJ MAHAL, INDIA

1653

Earth and us

A house carved out of solid stone in Cappadocia, Turkey, grins a gap-toothed smile! Around 5 million years ago, fiery clouds poured down from nearby volcanoes and covered the landscape in a thick layer of hot ash. Over time, the ash cooled and hardened into igneous rock. Homes like these have been hollowed out of the hard rock here since the days of ancient Rome. The rooms connect to one another with stairs, tunnels, and passageways.

Stone tech [Processed rocks]

We still live in the Stone Age! Look around you—everything that isn't made from a plant or animal (like paper, cotton, or leather) has been dug out of the ground. Metal, glass, microchips, and pottery all come from rocks. By learning how to extract raw materials from rocks and minerals, we have built the modern world.

Limestone

The mineral in limestone is calcium carbonate. Limestone is used to harden cement and plaster, and it makes whitewash white. But that's not all this useful rock does.

Ceramic tiles
Pulverized limestone powder is sometimes used to make ceramic tiles, since it is tough and widely available.

Minerals in our lives

Materials purified from the minerals in rocks are essential to modern life. They include all the metals in the objects around you, from cooking pots to circuits in your cell phone.

Diapers
Microscopic grains of pure calcium carbonate are rolled onto the fabric of diapers. The grains allow air in and out but keep liquids from leaking.

Lead

Lead occurs in the mineral galena. About 4.4 million tons of lead are mined each year, most of which is used in car batteries.

Iron
Found in the iron oxide minerals hematite and magnetite, iron is cheap to extract. Most iron is turned into steel for building.

Copper

Up to 22 million tons of copper are extracted per year. Copper is used for electrical wiring and plumbing pipes.

Strong iron
Limestone is added to the furnaces that purify iron from rocky ores. The limestone removes impurities that weaken the metal.

Salt
Salt is an important industrial chemical. It is also used to keep roads free of ice and to preserve food.

Clays

Clay minerals have a wide range of uses, including in pottery items and ceramic materials.

On average, each person on Earth uses over 2.2 tons of iron per year

Toothpaste
Finely ground calcium carbonate from limestone is added to toothpaste. The rock dust gently scrapes and polishes your teeth.

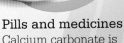

Pills and medicines
Calcium carbonate is harmless if swallowed. Complex carbon-based medicines are mixed into it to form pills.

Sand

The most common mineral is silica, or silicon dioxide, found in sand and quartz. The sand-filled hourglass was an early clock; today's quartz watches count time with vibrating crystals.

Glass
The most common use for sand is in the manufacture of transparent glass—an ancient process we've been using for 4,000 years.

Microchips
Computer chips are made from wafers of pure silicon, just 0.03 inches (0.75 mm) thick. Each wafer is a single flat crystal.

Optical fibers
Flexible tubes that carry Internet traffic and telecommunications are made from high-grade silica glass.

Reinforced concrete
The toughest concrete is strengthened with steel bars. Concrete contains limestone and sand, and carbon makes the steel superstrong.

Photovoltaic panels
Solar cells use silicon semiconductors to convert sunlight into electricity. They power everything from calculators to spacecraft.

Carbon

Pure carbon comes out of the ground in coal, graphite, or diamond. Other carbon minerals make up crude oil. Huge industries are devoted to collecting these valuable minerals.

Pencil lead
Graphite is a soft, slippery form of carbon, used for pencil lead (it's not really lead!), batteries, car brake linings, and lubricants.

Carbon fibers
Fine fibers of carbon are mixed with plastics to make a strong but superlight material. It is in race cars, aircraft wings, and sports equipment.

Plastic
Plastic, one of the most widely used materials in the world, is made from the carbon-based minerals in crude oil.

Crayons
Carbon-rich oil and waxes make crayons smooth. Similar waxes are used in candles and lipsticks.

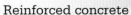
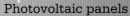

Remarkab

roc

* When do house-size rocks fly through the air?

* How do giant dragonflies get trapped in stone?

* Where are robot rovers studying alien rocks?

e

cks

All-star rocks [Gallery]

Too much of our Earth is covered in concrete. But underneath that human-made veneer is an amazing variety of rocks. The closer you look at a rock, the more you'll find out about its makeup and history.

115: the number of types of rock

Igneous rocks

These crystalline rocks sometimes contain valuable metals and priceless gems. In some igneous rocks, such as basalt, the crystals may be microscopic, but in others, such as pegmatite, they can grow to several feet long.

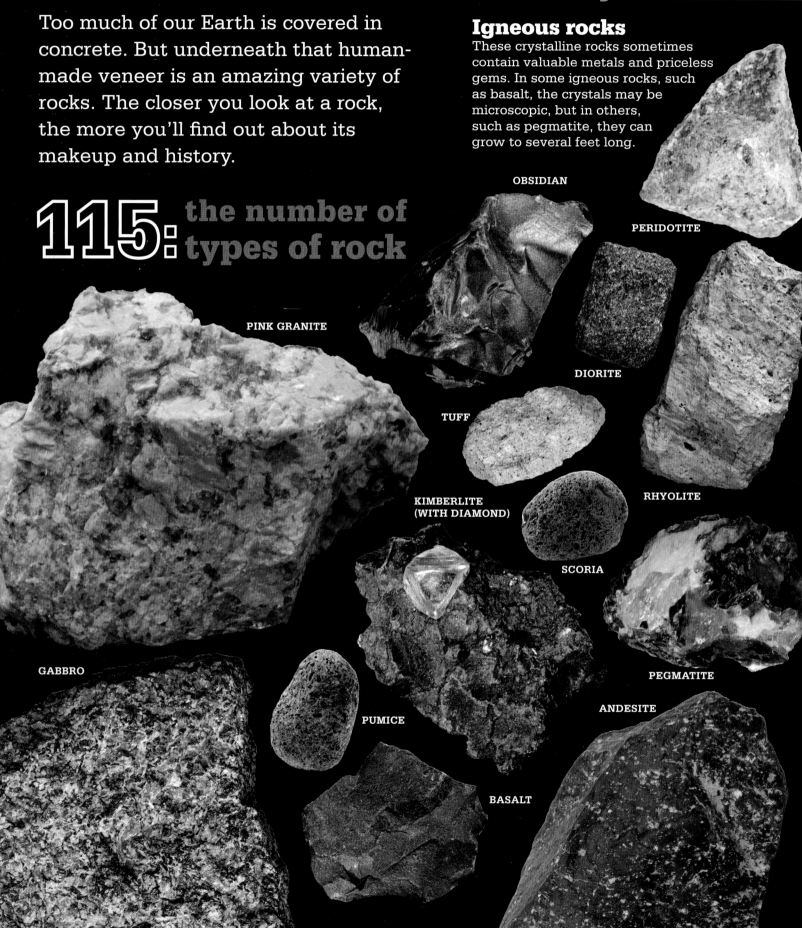

OBSIDIAN

PERIDOTITE

PINK GRANITE

DIORITE

TUFF

RHYOLITE

KIMBERLITE (WITH DIAMOND)

SCORIA

GABBRO

PEGMATITE

PUMICE

ANDESITE

BASALT

Sedimentary rocks

The particles that make up these rocks range in size from tiny grains in limestone to the pebble-size fragments found in conglomerate rocks. Flint has a glassy appearance, while rock salt is crystalline.

FLINT

IRONSTONE

CONGLOMERATE

SANDSTONE

BRECCIA

HALITE (ROCK SALT)

LIMESTONE

Metamorphic rocks

These rocks bear little resemblance to the rocks from which they form—compare metamorphic quartzite to sedimentary sandstone, from which it is made. Metamorphic rocks may have bands, as in the migmatite sample below.

AMPHIBOLITE

GNEISS

SLATE

SCHIST

MARBLE

HORNFELS

QUARTZITE

MIGMATITE

Recycling rocks [Dynamic

Nothing on Earth lasts forever—not even solid rock! Over millions of years, water, weather, and the planet's internal pressure and heat gradually destroy old rocks and reuse their minerals to make new rocks. This constant recycling is known as the rock cycle.

The rock cycle

Earth has been recycling rocks for billions of years, using the same materials to make and remake rocks in an endless cycle. The mineral crystals you can see in a rock today were almost certainly part of a completely different type of rock sometime in the past.

Power supply

The rock cycle is driven mainly by heat. Earth's hot interior melts rock into magma, which erupts from volcanoes as lava but also pushes up on the solid surface rock, making it buckle and crack. Energy from the Sun heats the atmosphere, creating weather, which wears away rock. Gravity also plays a part, by changing one rock type to another.

SOLAR ENERGY

Weather, which fragments rocks

Magma making new igneous rocks

VOLCANIC HEAT

Gravity, which squeezes rocks underground

GRAVITY

Sedimentary rock weathering and re-forming

Sedimentary rock squeezing into metamorphic rock

METAMORPHIC ROCKS

Metamorphic rock melting into igneous rock

Metamorphic rock metamorphosing again

Pressure cooker

Heat and pressure can change rocks without melting them first. This is called metamorphism (see pages 54–55). The rocks are squeezed by the movement of Earth's plates and the pull of gravity, then baked by rising magma bubbles.

MARBLE

SLATE

SCHIST

Metamorphic rocks

Marble is a metamorphic rock formed from limestone. Slate forms when shale is crushed and baked. So does schist, at much higher temperatures.

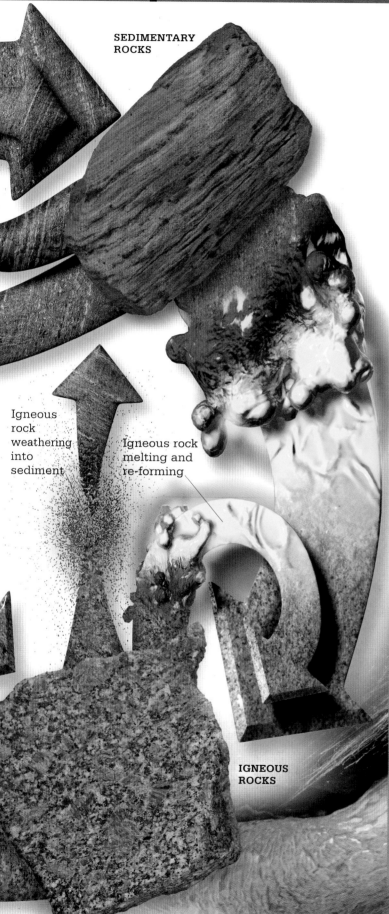

SEDIMENTARY ROCKS

Igneous rock weathering into sediment

Igneous rock melting and re-forming

IGNEOUS ROCKS

The daily grind

On Earth's surface, rocks take a beating. Rivers, waves, and glaciers wear them down; chemicals in rainwater attack them; and frost, temperature changes, and tree roots break them apart. This relentless destruction is called weathering.

Sedimentary rocks
Weathered rock grains build up as layers of sand, mud, and other sediments. These layers form new sedimentary rocks (see pages 40–41).

SANDSTONE

LIMESTONE

CONGLOMERATE

Around and around

This diagram shows the rock cycle. There are three ways of transforming rock: melting and cooling into igneous rock, squeezing and baking into metamorphic rock, or weathering into sedimentary rock. Any rock can be changed into any new type or can even be re-formed as another version of the same type.

Meltdown

Intense heat below the ground melts the rocks of the lower crust and upper mantle, turning them into magma. As magma rises toward the surface, it cools and forms new igneous rocks (see pages 36–37).

Igneous rocks
Obsidian and basalt form from magma that erupts onto the surface as lava. Gabbro forms when magma solidifies underground.

OBSIDIAN

GABBRO

BASALT

Igneous rocks

Taking their name from the Latin word *igneus*, these rocks are also known as fire rocks. And they are truly born of fire—they form when magma or lava, the molten rock that comes from deep inside Earth, cools and crystallizes.

Sharp stones

Obsidian is one of the few igneous rocks with no crystals at all. It cools so rapidly, it forms a natural dark glass. Obsidian cracks into pieces with extremely sharp edges and can be made into knives. Surgeons use obsidian scalpels to make the finest cuts.

Ghoulish glass
This fearsome obsidian blade was used by priests in ancient Mexico to sacrifice people by cutting out their hearts.

Basalt

Dark and moody looking, basalt is by far the most abundant lava rock on Earth—it's found everywhere, especially on the ocean floor.

What it is	Hard rock made in volcanic eruptions
Surface	Dark and rough, with tiny crystal grains
Main uses	Building stones, paving, cobblestones

Tough stuff
Too hard to be worn away by water, basalt columns in Iceland create the lip of a waterfall.

Pegmatite

Unmistakable pegmatite has enormous crystals. These grow large because water mixed into magma keeps the cooling rock bathed in fresh minerals. Pegmatite contains many rare metals, such as tungsten and lithium, and is an important source of gemstones.

Gemstone power
The big crystal in this pegmatite is euclase. It formed from an emerald soaked in water for millions of years.

What it is	Pale pinkish rock formed underground
Surface	Rough, with large crystal grains
Main uses	Source of metals and gemstones

Pumice

Like a rocky sponge, pumice is a foamy volcanic glass full of tiny bubbles and pores. It forms when gas-filled lava gushes out of a volcano.

What it is	Pale gray to black volcanic rock
Surface	Rough but soft, with no visible crystals
Main uses	Scrubbing stones, lightweight concrete

Spongy floater
A lump of obsidian sinks in water, but because it is full of holes, the pumice floats!

Peridotite

This is the rock that makes up the upper part of Earth's mantle. We get to see it when it is brought to the surface on a hot tide of upward-rushing magma. One variety contains diamonds.

What it is	Dark green to black mantle rock
Surface	Large, speckled crystal grains
Main uses	Source of chromium and diamonds

Metal source
The rock's green color comes mainly from minerals containing the metal chromium.

Granite

This is the most common rock under our feet. As it cools from sticky magma deep underground, it forms immense lumps called batholiths (see page 37). Some of them are hundreds of miles across.

What it is	Mottled pink, whitish, gray, or black rock formed underground
Surface	Rough, with a range of crystal sizes and colors
Main uses	Building stones, paving, statues, countertops

70%
of Earth's land is made of granite

Construction stone
Granite is one of the best building stones. Its big crystals produce an impressive polished finish.

Volcanic action [Hot rocks]

Volcanoes demonstrate the awesome power of our planet. These fiery fountains channel molten rock from deep inside Earth up to the surface, constantly creating fresh igneous rock and renewing Earth's crust.

Lava bomb
The most explosive volcanic eruptions throw out lumps of molten rock called bombs. As they fly through the air, lava bombs cool into solid torpedoes of rock. Most bombs are small, but some are as big as houses.

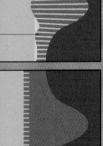

Moving lava   Cooling pool   Columns

1 Hot liquid
Red-hot lava flows across the land, forming lakes in hollow areas.

2 Cool down
The lava cools and gets stickier. Eventually, it stops flowing altogether.

3 Cracking up
As the lava turns solid, vertical cracks form, creating columns of hard rock.

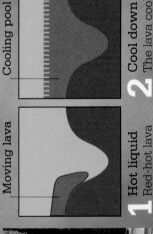

The Giant's Causeway
Magma that erupts from a volcano onto the surface as lava may cool into hexagonal columns. The Giant's Causeway in Northern Ireland has more than 40,000 such columns.

Ash figure
Easter Island, in the Pacific Ocean, is famous for its *moai*, or stone statues. They were carved centuries ago from tuff, an igneous rock formed from volcanic ash.

Volcano
Magma is less dense than the surrounding solid rock is, so it rises toward the surface. It collects in a magma chamber, but eventually the pressure in the chamber becomes so great that the volcano erupts. As lava, it spreads across the land, scorching and burning all it touches. Igneous rock that forms when lava cools on the surface is known as extrusive rock. Intrusive rock is formed by magma solidifying under the ground.

Vent
(opening)

Ash clouds
and gas

Village
People often live near volcanoes despite the danger, because volcanic minerals make the soil fertile and good for farming.

Lava lake

Dike
Liquid magma that pushes up into vertical cracks cools to form walls of rock known as dikes.

Feeder pipe
The vent of a volcano is fed by a long tube that pipes molten rock up from deeper reservoirs of magma.

Magma chamber
An underground magma chamber can grow larger as it melts the surrounding crustal rock. The magma in the chamber may also cool to form a vast, domelike rock called a batholith.

Laccolith
This dome of magma forms between two layers of older rock. It will eventually push the surface up to form a small hill.

Sill
Magma that fills horizontal cracks in older rock forms sills. Sills cool into medium-grained igneous rocks such as dolerite (see page 102).

Ship Rock
Ship Rock, in New Mexico, is the remains of an ancient volcano frozen in time. Long dikes, which formed when the volcano was active, spread out from the hardened volcanic core.

Half Dome
This famous mass of granite in Yosemite, CA, is an ancient batholith that has been exposed at the surface by millions of years of erosion.

Facing fire
This brave explorer could not survive without his protective heat suit as he descends into Marum's crater, on volcanic Ambrym Island in the Pacific Ocean. As the lava boils and churns, temperatures in the crater reach 2,000°F (1,100°C).

Horrible history

Volcanoes have been spilling red-hot lava, ash, and toxic gases for millions of years. But only when we started to record details of eruptions did we begin to understand these rock factories and the awesome forces that power them.

1600 BCE The mythical city of Atlantis may have been real, and devastated by one of the largest volcanic eruptions ever, on the Greek island of Thera.

ca. 20 BCE The ancient Romans believed that Mount Etna, on the island of Sicily, was the forge of Vulcan, the blacksmith of the gods.

AUG. 24, 79 CE Historian Pliny the Younger watched the volcano Vesuvius, near Naples, Italy, destroy the Roman cities of Pompeii and Herculaneum.

OBJECTS FOUND IN VESUVIUS'S ASH

AUG. 26, 1883 Indonesia's Krakatau volcano exploded, causing the deaths of 36,417 people. The effects of the eruption were felt around the globe.

MAR. 20, 2010 A towering ash plume from Iceland's Eyjafjallajökull volcano disrupted air traffic across Europe, stranding thousands of people for days.

EYJAFJALLAJÖKULL'S ASH PLUME

The Krakatau eruption was the loudest *BOOM* in history, heard 3,000 miles (4,800 km) away

Layered rocks [Fossil

Many sedimentary rocks are made from fragments of other, older rocks that have been broken down by weathering (see page 33) and turned into sediment. The fossils found in sedimentary rocks tell us about life on Earth millions of years ago.

Rock to rock

Weathered rock fragments are washed down rivers to the sea. As they travel, the fragments gradually wear down even more, often until they are reduced to tiny grains. The grains eventually settle on the riverbed or seafloor as sediment. Thus, the debris from weathering becomes raw material for new sedimentary rock.

Rainwater

Ice

1 Transport
Wind and rain carry weathered rocks into rivers. The fast-flowing water transports the rock fragments toward the coast.

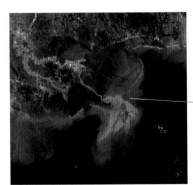

Sediment

2 Sedimentation
Near the coast, a river widens, flows more slowly, and begins to drop its cargo of rock grains. Most of the sediment is deposited just off the coast.

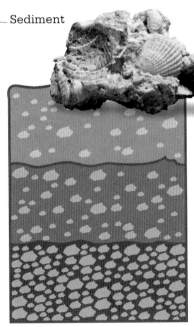

3 New rock formation
Sediment layers build up. Over time, the weight of the layers above squeezes water out of the sediments below, compacting or cementing the grains together into new rock.

Sedimentary canyon
Thin layers of sediment build up to form thicker deposits called beds. Alternating beds made of different sediments can give rock the look of a colorful layer cake. Wind and water may carve the beds into amazing shapes and patterns, as seen here in Antelope Canyon in Arizona.

keepers]

How old?
The 17th-century geologist Nicolas Steno understood that sediments are always laid down in horizontal beds. He realized that the beds at the tops of sedimentary rock formations are the youngest and those at the bottom are the oldest.

Fossil factor
Steno was one of the pioneers in the science of geology.

NICOLAS STENO
Geologist

Lived   January 1, 1638–
               November 25, 1686

Famous for   Understanding
               sedimentary rock layers

Cast in stone
Many people in the 17th century believed that fossils grew inside rocks. However, Nicolas Steno correctly suggested that fossils are the remnants of ancient animals and plants preserved in stone.

1 Life in the past
Sedimentary rocks often contain fossils, because they formed beneath rivers and oceans that were rich in aquatic life, like this ancient fish.

2 Death of a fish
When the fish died, its body sank and came to rest on the seafloor. Sediments settling on the seabed began to cover the dead fish.

3 Preservation
As the fish was buried in sediment, its softer parts decomposed. Harder body parts, such as bones, absorbed minerals, which helped preserve them.

4 Fossilization
As the sediment hardened into rock, the remains became fossilized. Millions of years later, weathering exposed the fossilized fish at the surface.

Dinosaur fossil wall
These fossilized dinosaur bones are among many preserved in a sloping rock formation at the Dinosaur National Monument in Utah. In the Jurassic period (199 to 145 million years ago), many dead dinosaurs floated down a river and became stuck on a sandbar, which eventually turned to rock.

Rocks as clocks [Fossils

Fossilized bones, shells, and other remains trapped inside solid rocks show us which plants and animals were alive when those rocks were soft sediments. By investigating fossils, scientists learn more about the history of life on Earth.

252 MYA   MASS EXTINCTION EVENT

The Great Dying
Fossils show that many life-forms have died out suddenly in mass extinctions. In the Great Dying, for example, 83 percent of all life disappeared.

Rock science
Scientists who study fossils are called paleontologists.

Fossil record
Geologists record the history of Earth on a timescale divided into eons, eras, and periods. Precambrian time produced few fossils; there are more from the Paleozoic era, since most major groups of life emerged then. Reptiles ruled the planet during the Mesozoic era. We are now in the Cenozoic era, also called the Age of Mammals.

375 MYA
Vertebrates (animals with backbones) began to leave the sea and adapt to life on land.

4 BYA (billion years ago)
The planet's oldest rocks date from 4.2 billion years ago.

450 MYA (million years ago)
Simple plants and animals moved onto land.

300 MYA
All of Earth's land was joined together in a single supercontinent called Pangaea.

• 4.6 BYA PRECAMBRIAN • 542 MYA   **PALEOZOIC**

| CAMBRIAN | ORDOVICIAN | SILURIAN | DEVONIAN | CARBONIFEROUS | PERMIAN |

Brachiopod (450 MYA)
The shells of these animals survive as fossils.

Crinoid (440 MYA)
This marine animal could attach itself to the seafloor.

Stromatolite (3 BYA)
These stony mounds are composed of millions of layers of ancient microbes and sediment.

Dragonfly (300 MYA)
These giant predatory insects patrolled prehistoric skies.

Sea pen (560 MYA)
The oldest animal fossils are of soft-bodied creatures like this one.

Trilobite (520 MYA)
This sea creature resembled a wood louse.

Rhabdoderma **(300 MYA)**
This early fish was an ancestor of the first land vertebrates.

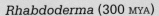

through time]

251–65 MYA
Mesozoic era
The best-known fossils are of dinosaurs, which lived in the Mesozoic. These reptiles were some of the largest animals ever to roam the planet. Flowering plants also began growing in this era.

TRICERATOPS
(70–65 MYA)

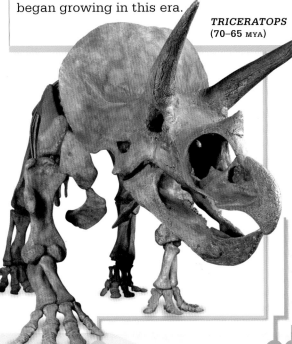

200,000 years ago
New arrival
The oldest fossils of modern humans are from Africa. Humans are relative newcomers to planet Earth—the whole of human existence covers just 0.02 percent of Earth's long history.

MODERN HUMAN	
Homo sapiens	
Scientific classification	Primate
Meaning of name	"Wise man"

65 MYA
The dinosaurs died in a mass extinction, leaving mammals and birds as Earth's biggest animals.

56 MYA
For a time, giant flightless hunting birds were the fiercest predators on land.

2.58 MYA
Earth became colder. Fossils from this time include woolly mammoths and rhinos, and saber-toothed tigers.

51 MYA	**MESOZOIC**			**65** MYA	**CENOZOIC**		**Present day**
TRIASSIC	JURASSIC	CRETACEOUS		PALEOGENE		NEOGENE	QUATERNARY

Crocodile (60 MYA)
This crocodile swam in ancient seas.

Future fossils
Will the "Age of Humans" create new types of fossil—perhaps from pottery, plastics, or concrete?

Saber-toothed tiger (2.5 MYA)
This fierce predator hunted mammoths and other large prey.

Scallop (22 MYA)
Fossils of these common seashells are found in Cenozoic rocks.

Feathered dinosaur (125 MYA)
Modern birds are related to two-legged dinosaurs.

Ammonite (200 MYA)
These free-swimming mollusks lived in all the oceans.

Trace fossil
Any trace of life can become a fossil—even a footprint or this ichthyosaur poop!

Megalodon **(1.5 MYA)**
This fossilized *megalodon* tooth came from the largest shark species that ever lived.

Sedimentary rocks [True

Most of the rocks that we see on Earth's surface are sedimentary. Take a walk along a beach, stopping to study the pebbles and look up at the cliffs. Whether the rocks are chalk, limestone, or sandstone, they are often rich in fossils, ready for examination by an amateur geologist.

The summit of Mount Everest was a limestone seabed 450 million years ago

Chalk

This rock is made from the shells of microscopic sea creatures. Most chalk was formed about 100 million years ago, when the oceans were much larger than they are today. Blackboard chalk was once made of this rock, but today it is made of gypsum.

Chalky heights

These tall Danish cliffs are made of chalk 400 feet (122 m) thick.

What it is	Soft, pale rock made in seabeds
Surface	Tiny grains; may contain fossils
Main uses	Cement, filling powder in pastes and foods

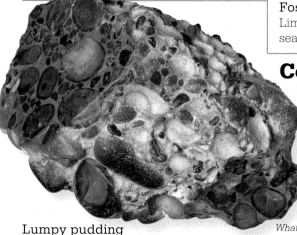

Lumpy pudding

This conglomerate is called pudding stone. It formed on an ancient beach where smooth pebbles were buried in sand.

Limestone

A very common rock, limestone is made of fragments of seashells and dead corals. The main mineral in it is calcium carbonate. Although limestone is hard, weak acids in rainwater slowly dissolve it.

What it is	Gray or yellow-brown seabed rock
Surface	Small or medium grains
Main uses	Cement, fertilizers, iron production

Fossils

Limestone is a good source of fossils of sea creatures, such as this limpet shell.

Conglomerate

These sedimentary rocks have the biggest grains. They are made of large fragments of several types of rock, all embedded in a smooth cement. Conglomerates contain round pebbles. Rocks with sharp fragments are called breccia.

What it is	Mixture of larger pebbles and stones, with fine-grained stone in between
Surface	Very large grains; no fossils
Main uses	Building stones

Blast powder

Dynamite contains a type of sandstone called diatomaceous earth. Without the powder made from this soft rock, the explosive would go off without warning. This rock's grains are the silica skeletons of diatoms, microscopic brown algae found in lakes and seas.

STICKS OF DYNAMITE

Sandstone

This hard stone is made from sand grains blown by winds into a desert or washed up on a beach. There are tiny pores, or holes, between the grains, which means that sandstone often holds water, gas, or oil.

What it is	Hard yellow-red rock
Surface	Small or medium grains
Main uses	Building and grinding stones

Pink palace

Sandstone can be carved into intricate shapes and designs, as seen at the Palace of the Winds in Jaipur, India.

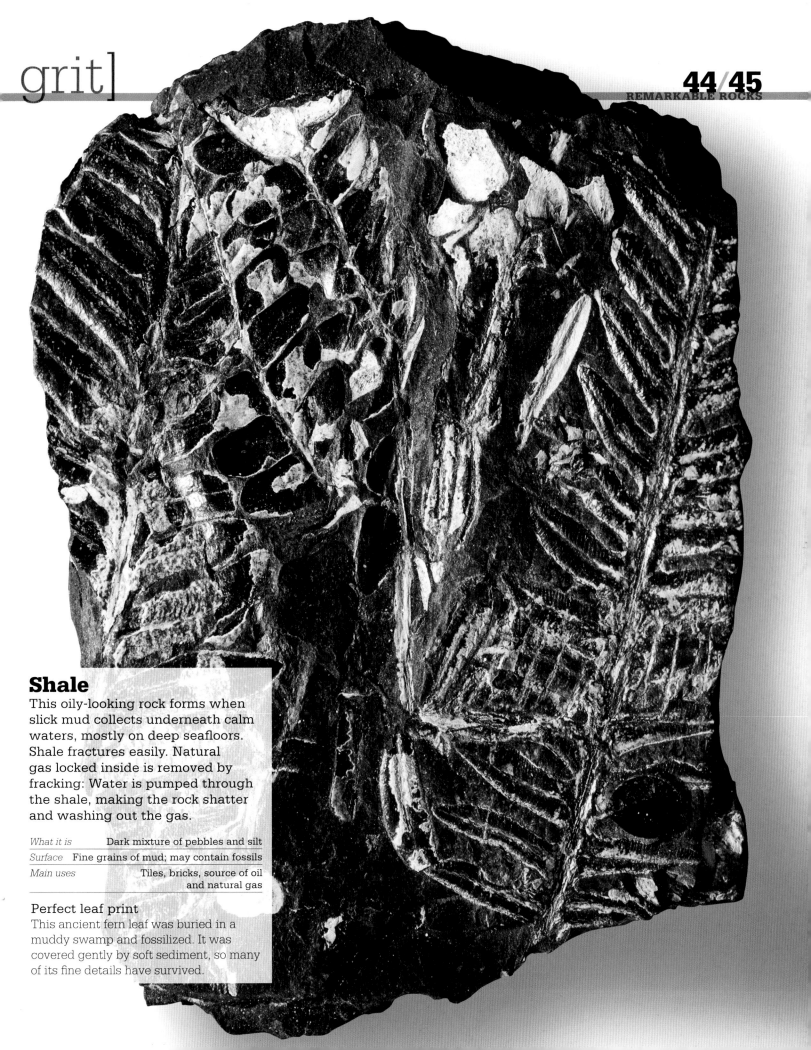

Shale

This oily-looking rock forms when slick mud collects underneath calm waters, mostly on deep seafloors. Shale fractures easily. Natural gas locked inside is removed by fracking: Water is pumped through the shale, making the rock shatter and washing out the gas.

What it is	Dark mixture of pebbles and silt
Surface	Fine grains of mud; may contain fossils
Main uses	Tiles, bricks, source of oil and natural gas

Perfect leaf print

This ancient fern leaf was buried in a muddy swamp and fossilized. It was covered gently by soft sediment, so many of its fine details have survived.

What a hoodoo!

Soft dawn light on Bryce Canyon, in Utah, shows off the lovely colors of the canyon's sedimentary rock layers. About 70 million years ago, the rocks were still loose sands on a shallow seabed. Over millions of years, they were compressed into solid rock. Today, the sandstone is being worn away by a relentless combination of weathering by rain and freezing and cracking by ice. This forms flat-topped buttes (above) and gnomelike bulges called hoodoos (left).

Water stones [Chemical

Some sedimentary rocks form when minerals dissolved in water turn into solid particles and settle out to form chemical sediments. This occurs as the water cools or evaporates away. Coal—almost pure carbon—is slightly different: It is the chemical residue of dead plants.

Hammer | Flint | Gunpowder | Frizzen | Trigger

RUSSIAN FLINTLOCK PISTOL, 1750

Coal

Coal comes from lush plants that grew in steamy swamps hundreds of millions of years ago. Dead plant remains sank and were buried. Over the years, they were gradually squeezed dry and turned into rock.

What it is	Organic chemical sediment
Surface	Crumbly and sooty to hard and glassy
Main uses	Burned to generate electricity and heat homes

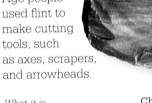

Fuel mine
Like wood, coal burns—but even hotter. It forms in layers called seams. Miners dig out the seams, deep underground (see page 50).

Flint

When mineral-rich water deposits quartz in cavities in limestone and chalk, pebblelike lumps called flint nodules are produced. If broken open, the nodules are dark and glassy inside. Their quartz crystals are so fine, they can be seen only with a microscope.

Cutting edge
Flint cracks into sharp-edged flakes. Stone Age people used flint to make cutting tools, such as axes, scrapers, and arrowheads.

What it is	Chemical sediment
Surface	Glassy, with no visible crystals
Main uses	Sharp-edged stone tools, ornaments, struck to light fires

Creating a spark

Flint is used as a striking stone for lighting fires. When struck with steel, it produces a shower of sparks. This property was used in early flintlock guns. Pulling the trigger brought a small piece of flint, held in a spring-loaded hammer, down onto a metal frizzen. The strike created a spark, which ignited a gunpowder charge.

36 feet (11 m): the length of the world's largest gypsum crystal

Ironstone

Banded ironstone records a big event in Earth's history— the period when algae added oxygen gas to the atmosphere for the first time, hundreds of millions of years ago.

Dark stripes
Oxygen released by microscopic algae in the ocean joined with dissolved iron, forming dark, metal-rich bands in ironstone.

What it is	Biochemical sediment
Surface	Fine grains
Main uses	Source of iron ore

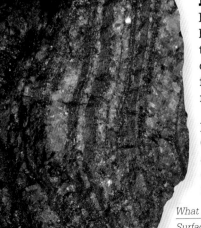

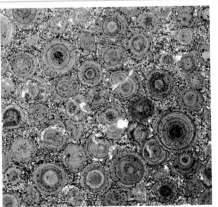

Oolitic limestone

This limestone looks like it contains fish eggs. The "eggs" are actually tiny balls of calcium carbonate, called ooids. The ooids form when calcium carbonate slowly settles out of warm seawater.

What it is	Chemical sediment
Surface	Contains rounded balls
Main uses	Polished ornaments

Ringed within
This slice of oolitic limestone shows layers of calcium carbonate inside the ooids.

Rock gypsum

Made mainly of the mineral gypsum
(see page 85), rock gypsum is an
evaporite—it forms from the residue
left behind when seawater or a salt
lake dries up. It occurs in thick beds,
interlayered with other sediments.
Alabaster, a brilliant white variety
of gypsum, is used in sculpture.

What it is	Evaporite chemical sediment
Surface	Fine grains, soft
Main uses	Plaster of Paris, drywall

Desert rose

This type of gypsum forms in hot
deserts. As water evaporates, the
mineral crystallizes around grains of
sand, forming flowerlike clusters.

When you switch on a light in your home, you are probably using electricity produced by burning coal, oil, or natural gas (also called methane). These naturally occurring fuels extracted from Earth's rocks are the remains of plants and animals that were buried around 300 million years ago— long before the time of the dinosaurs.

Carbon dioxide collected from the air by plants

Mining machines extracting coal

Buried, pressed, and heated plants

Coal

Drill tapping oil and gas from underground reservoirs

Fossil fuels

Living things absorb carbon and use it to build their bodies. When buried at depths of up to 3.5 miles (5.6 km) and baked at 212°F (100°C) for millions of years, their carbon-rich remains may fossilize and turn into coal, oil, and natural gas. We call these fuels fossil fuels.

Burial and fuel formation

Dead plants built up in prehistoric tropical swamps, and the remains of tiny marine organisms formed layers on the seafloor. Over time, the plants slowly changed into coal, and the marine organisms into oil and gas.

Extraction

Coal is dug from deep underground tunnels or from huge pits on the surface called open-cast mines. Oil and gas are extracted by drilling down to reserves trapped between rock layers. Pressure forces the oil and gas to the surface.

Taichung power plant, Taiwan
The world's largest coal-fired plant, Taichung, produces enough electricity to power several million homes. It is also the world's most polluting plant, emitting 39 million tons of carbon dioxide per year.

23.1

18.9

Oil use by region, 2011
(millions of barrels per day)

8

3.4

Heat

6.3

Sunlight

28.3

11.1
(1965)

World oil use
(millions of barrels per day)

88
(2011)

Power plants
burning coal and natural gas

Carbon dioxide
gas trapping heat

Using fossil fuels
Burning fossil fuels releases the energy stored inside them. We harness this energy to generate electricity and to power our vehicles. As fossil fuels burn, they release carbon dioxide gas into Earth's atmosphere.

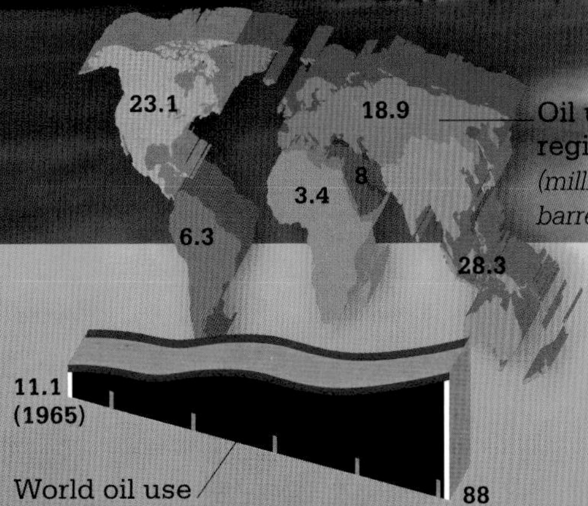

Fuel reserves
The amount of fossil fuels we use is rising—we now use nearly 8 times more oil than we did about 50 years ago. Earth's fossil fuel supplies will run out one day, so we need to find alternative energy sources.

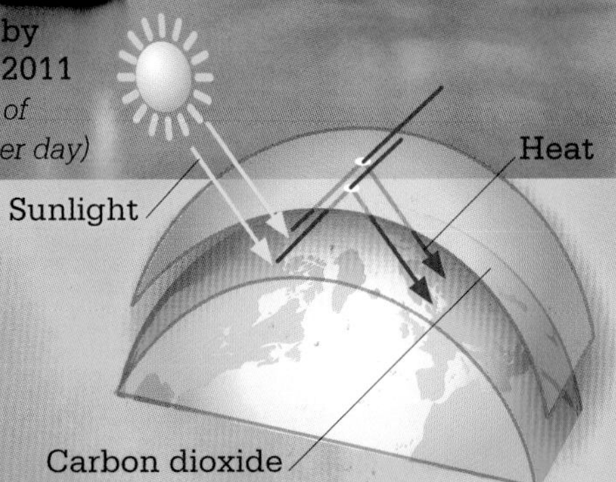

Climate change
Each year, burning fossil fuels adds a huge amount of carbon dioxide— 3,500 times the weight of Egypt's Great Pyramid—to the air. This gas traps the Sun's heat, warming the planet and altering the climate.

Caves [Rocky hollows]

Caves are naturally occurring underground holes, usually carved out by flowing water. They may contain strange rock formations and some weird-looking animals. Even the people who explore caves have a funny name—*spelunkers*!

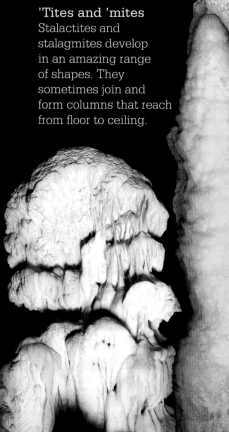

Stalactite
A stalactite clings to a cave ceiling. It holds on "tite"!

Rock sculptures

Water running through limestone dissolves carbonate minerals in the rock. When this mineral-rich water trickles into a cave, it can create sculpturelike structures called stalactites and stalagmites.

1 Drippy start
As mineral-filled water drips through a cave ceiling, it begins to form a solid deposit of carbonate minerals.

2 Slow growth
The carbonate minerals build up over centuries and form a hanging stalactite. Drops that fall to the floor create a matching stalagmite.

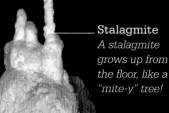

Stalagmite
A stalagmite grows up from the floor, like a "mite-y" tree!

Rock rings
A horizontal slice of a stalactite reveals how it formed. Delicate bands, like tree rings, show how it slowly grew, layer by layer.

'Tites and 'mites
Stalactites and stalagmites develop in an amazing range of shapes. They sometimes join and form columns that reach from floor to ceiling.

Cave dwellers

Animals that have adapted to living in caves spend their whole lives in complete darkness. Called troglobites, these animals are often ghostly white. Many cave creatures are blind, with small eyes; some have no eyes at all.

Texas blind salamander
This amphibian can reach 6 in. (13 cm) in length. Its bloodred gills absorb oxygen from water.

Snottite
Goopy bacteria colonies called snottites make superstrong acid, which can dissolve solid rock.

Blindfish
The eyeless blindfish can detect a cave's walls using water-current sensors along its sides.

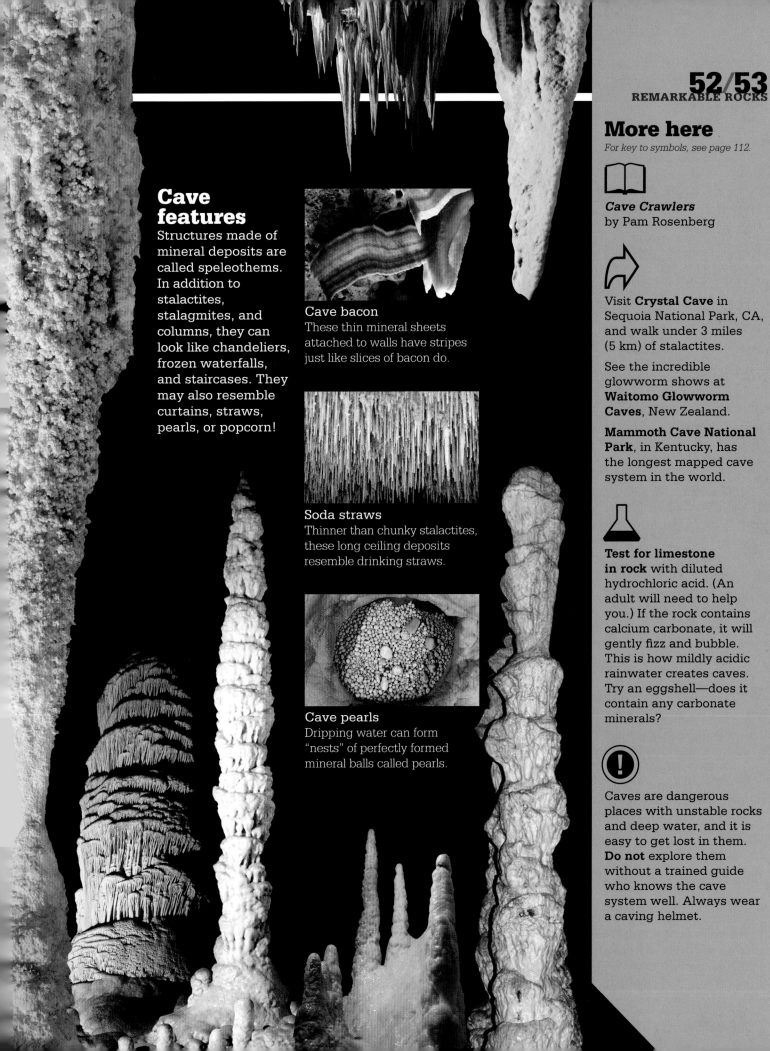

Cave features

Structures made of mineral deposits are called speleothems. In addition to stalactites, stalagmites, and columns, they can look like chandeliers, frozen waterfalls, and staircases. They may also resemble curtains, straws, pearls, or popcorn!

Cave bacon
These thin mineral sheets attached to walls have stripes just like slices of bacon do.

Soda straws
Thinner than chunky stalactites, these long ceiling deposits resemble drinking straws.

Cave pearls
Dripping water can form "nests" of perfectly formed mineral balls called pearls.

More here

For key to symbols, see page 112.

Cave Crawlers
by Pam Rosenberg

Visit **Crystal Cave** in Sequoia National Park, CA, and walk under 3 miles (5 km) of stalactites.

See the incredible glowworm shows at **Waitomo Glowworm Caves**, New Zealand.

Mammoth Cave National Park, in Kentucky, has the longest mapped cave system in the world.

Test for limestone in rock with diluted hydrochloric acid. (An adult will need to help you.) If the rock contains calcium carbonate, it will gently fizz and bubble. This is how mildly acidic rainwater creates caves. Try an eggshell—does it contain any carbonate minerals?

Caves are dangerous places with unstable rocks and deep water, and it is easy to get lost in them. **Do not** explore them without a trained guide who knows the cave system well. Always wear a caving helmet.

Changing stone

The Earth groans and shudders as vast slabs of crustal rock called plates (see page 88) move over its surface. Deep underground, the heat and pressure caused by this motion start to metamorphose, or transform, rocks. This is how, for example, dull limestone can change into beautiful, creamy marble.

Marble memorial
The Lincoln Memorial in Washington, D.C., honors one of the greatest US presidents, Abraham Lincoln (1809–65). It was built using white marble from across the United States. Millions visit this enduring symbol every year.

Building exterior (Colorado)

Washington, D.C.

Base (Tennessee)

Statue (Georgia)

SOME SOURCES OF MEMORIAL MARBLE

Making marble

Marble forms by contact metamorphism, which occurs when limestone is baked by a nearby magma chamber (see page 37). Another type of metamorphism, dynamic metamorphism, happens where the plates of Earth's crust meet and exert huge pressure as they rub together. Regional metamorphism occurs where plates collide and force up mountain ranges.

Quarry town of Marble, CO
The town was founded in 1899, after high-quality marble was found in the area. Yule marble is still quarried there today, and exported worldwide.

Polisher
High-quality marble like Yule marble can be polished to a glossy shine. In the past, this was a long, tiring job done by hand, often by young children. Today, most polishing is done by machine.

Monster machines
Some of the marble for the Lincoln Memorial was cut from steep cliffs above Yule Creek near Marble, CO, in the early 20th century. Huge, electrically powered cranes moved the stone.

Marble flower

Completed in 1986, the Bahá'í House of Worship, in India, is shaped like a lotus flower. It has 27 freestanding "petals" clad with white marble quarried from Mount Pentelicus in Greece. Pentelic marble has been used to adorn prestigious buildings for thousands of years, including the ancient acropolis in Athens.

BAHÁ'Í HOUSE OF WORSHIP, INDIA

Metamorphic process

Heat alters the minerals inside rocks and creates new crystal grains. Pressure pushes the minerals into thin layers. The amount of heat and pressure to which the minerals are exposed determines what type of metamorphic rock forms (see left).

Parent rocks
The original rock that is metamorphosed is called the parent rock. Some metamorphic rocks form from only one type of parent rock.

INCREASING TEMPERATURE

Only high temperature applied

HORNFELS

INCREASING METAMORPHISM

LOW

SHALE

INCREASING PRESSURE

SLATE

SCHIST

GNEISS

HIGH

MIGMATITE

Only high pressure applied

BLUESCHIST

PARENT ROCK		METAMORPHIC ROCK
LIMESTONE	→	MARBLE
SANDSTONE	→	QUARTZITE
GRANITE	→	GNEISS
COAL	→	ANTHRACITE
SHALE	→	SLATE

Metamorphic rocks

One of the oldest rock formations on Earth is metamorphic. The Acasta Gneiss in northern Canada is about 4 billion years old—nearly as old as Earth itself. It contains quartz and feldspar, probably derived from metamorphosed granite.

Quartzite

Gritty quartzite is a tough, durable rock that forms when sandstone is baked hard inside Earth. The heat melts the quartz sand grains, which recrystallize into larger grains that interlock tightly with no gaps between them.

Bow Fiddle rock

Quartzite often rises above the landscape—as it does in this impressive formation in Scotland—because it wears away more slowly than its surroundings do.

What it is	Metamorphosed sandstone
Surface	Medium-size crystals, like lumps of sugar
Main uses	Stone Age tools, railroads, highways

Serpentinite

The surface of this shiny green rock resembles snakeskin. Serpentinite forms when hot water is forced through the rocks of Earth's mantle, deep beneath the ocean floor. As its name suggests, it contains a lot of the mineral serpentine.

Carving stone

With its soft and oily texture, serpentinite is easy to carve. The Inuit people of Canada traditionally shape serpentinite into statues (left) and lamps.

What it is	Metamorphosed mantle rock
Surface	Coarse grains; looks oily
Main uses	Decoration

Slate

This dull-colored stone forms when sedimentary shale rock is buried and then exposed to relatively low pressures and temperatures. Slate is not as hard as other metamorphic rocks are. It breaks into flat slabs and is used for tiles and countertops.

What it is	Metamorphosed shale
Surface	Very fine grains; splits into sheets
Main uses	Roof tiles, floor tiles, countertops

Rock leaves

When tapped gently with a hammer, slate breaks into thin, flat leaves, or sheets, like the pages of a book. The word *slate* comes from an Old High German word meaning "to split."

Lightning stone

This glassy stone is created when lightning strikes sandy beaches and dunes. The heat makes sand grains fuse together to form knobby, hollow tubes of rock known as fulgurites.

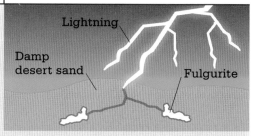

Changed in a flash

Lightning has no trouble reaching the 3,270°F (1,800°C) needed to melt sand. The fulgurite tubes branch out under the sand's surface like tree roots.

Gneiss

It's hard to tell which rock turns into gneiss, which forms when one section of Earth's crust sinks beneath another, crumpling and stewing the rocks it contains. Gneiss is easily recognizable from its large mineral grains arranged in dark and light bands.

What it is	Very old metamorphic rock
Surface	Medium and large crystals
Main uses	Building

Striped stone

As gneiss forms, the heated minerals rearrange themselves into stripes.

White marble
Made mostly of calcite, pure marble is snowy white, with a faint sparkle.

Marble

This beautiful rock is formed when limestone is buried deep within Earth's crust or is baked by an upsurge of hot magma. Marble is soft enough to carve, so it is ideal for making sculptures. It is also tough enough to use on floors and as the walls of buildings.

What it is	Metamorphosed limestone
Surface	Medium-coarse, sugary grains
Main uses	Building, decoration

The many faces of marble

Impurities in marble produce an amazing range of colors and patterns. Marble can be polished to a gentle shine, so it is widely used as a decorative stone.

3,000:

the number of types of marble

Space rocks [Alien invaders]

Rocks called meteorites fall to Earth from space. These rocks either have been knocked off other planets or are lumps of debris left over from the formation of the solar system billions of years ago. Space missions have also sampled and analyzed alien rocks.

ChemCam
A laser vaporizes a rock, and ChemCam analyzes the vapor to determine the rock's chemical makeup.

Meteors and meteorites

The streaks of light you see flashing across the night sky are meteors—small space rocks and flecks of grit that burn up in Earth's atmosphere. Meteorites are larger rocks that make it to the ground. About 19,000 meteorites hit Earth each year.

Meteor shower

Meteors are also known as shooting stars. Every year, there are spectacular meteor "showers." The biggest showers are in August and November.

Metal meteorite

Most meteorites are stony meteorites, which are similar in composition to the rocks of Earth's mantle. Iron meteorites (right) are composed mainly of the metals iron and nickel, plus a small amount of minerals.

Comet probe

Scientists don't always wait for space rocks to land on Earth. In 2005, the NASA space probe *Deep Impact* flew next to a comet and fired a spike into it to learn what it was made of.

Deep Impact probe

Alien rocks

The Apollo astronauts brought back 842 pounds (382 kg) of rock from the Moon. These rock samples are similar to igneous rocks in Earth's crust. This suggests that the Moon was formed from a chunk of Earth or was born at the same time as Earth. We also have rocks from Mars to study.

Apollo 11 mission
In 1969, Buzz Aldrin set up this seismometer on the surface of the Moon. It sent back information about "moonquakes" to Earth.

Sample Analysis at Mars (SAM)
Curiosity has a drill and a scoop for collecting samples and delivering them to its sophisticated onboard laboratory.

Curiosity rover
This robotic vehicle landed on the surface of Mars in 2012. It is looking for signs of life on the red planet. No one actually expects Curiosity to find any living things, but the rocks of Mars—just like Earth's—may contain traces of ancient life-forms.

More here

For key to symbols, see page 112.

near-Earth object (NEO) meteor shower **Moon rock Allan Hills 84001** Peekskill meteorite car **Chicxulub crater** *NEAR Shoemaker*

NOVA: Ultimate Mars Challenge (PBS, 2012) is a documentary about the Curiosity rover: how NASA landed it on Mars, and what experiments it will do on the red planet's rocks.

The **American Museum of Natural History**, in New York City, NY, displays the largest meteorite ever found in the US, the iron Willamette meteorite. It weighs 15.5 tons.

Visit one of the world's most impressive meteor impact sites, **Meteor Crater** in Arizona.

Find a dark place to watch the glorious Perseids and Geminids in the night skies. These meteor showers occur in mid-July to August and December, respectively, and are caused when Earth passes through debris left by comets and asteroids.

Magnific
min

* How can you make your own crystals?

* How do astronauts use silver?

* Why do sparklers glow?

ent

erals

Marvelous minerals

Tiny mineral crystals are building blocks for rocks, but minerals also occur on their own as larger formations. Most minerals solidify from a hot liquid soup of ingredients. Each one differs in its shape and chemical makeup, but the end result is often magnificent.

GALENA

MIMETITE

Native elements

A mineral that consists of a single element in its pure state—that is, uncombined with other elements— is called a native element. These metals and nonmetals are some of the oldest-known elements.

Compound minerals

By far the most common minerals are compounds (see page 16). They form when two or more elements join together chemically to make a new solid substance.

CARNALLITE

FELDSPAR

COPPER

DIAMOND (CARBON)

AQUAMARINE

KÄMMERERITE

SILVER

OLIVINE

GRAPHITE (CARBON)

APOPHYLLITE

GOLD

SULFUR

IRON

DIOPTASE

LAZURITE

MAGNETITE

WULFENITE

CHALCEDONY
QUARTZ

FLUORITE

ORPIMENT

TOURMALINE

EUCLASE

MALACHITE

ADAMITE

PYRITE

SMITHSONITE

SPHALERITE

HEULANDITE

ARAGONITE

STILBITE

COBALTOAN
DOLOMITE

GYROLITE

DIOPTASE

TIGEREYE

EMERALD

HEMATITE

KYANITE

OPAL

CALCITE

GYPSUM

MOLYBDENITE

SCOLECITE

TOPAZ ON
QUARTZ

MARCASITE (WITH GALENA SPHERES)

ARAGONITE

OKENITE

WAVELLITE

RHODOCHROSITE

CALCITE AND FLUORITE

BARITE

CUPRO-AUSTINITE

ALBITE

TOURMALINE

STIBNITE

PYROMORPHITE

HALITE (ROCK SALT)

HEMATITE

CITRINE

VARISCITE

PENTAGONITE

Crystals [Inside

An essential feature of all minerals is their crystal structure. Each individual crystal has its own particular shape, formed by regular, repeating units of atoms. Minerals also have large-scale properties, which are easier to see and can help identify them.

Hardness

Some minerals are harder than others. Comparing the hardness of two minerals that look similar is a great way to identify them. A mineral's hardness can also be compared to the hardness of everyday items.

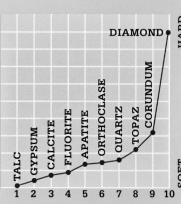

Mohs scale of hardness
This scale gives a number to a mineral's hardness based on which of the ten common minerals above can scratch it. Harder minerals will leave scratches on softer ones.

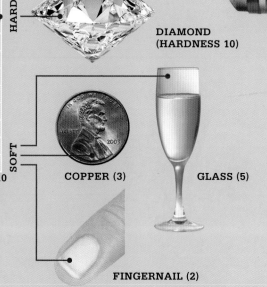

DIAMOND
(HARDNESS 10)

COPPER (3)

GLASS (5)

FINGERNAIL (2)

Crystal shapes

Crystals take on different shapes, based on the conditions in which they grow. The shape of a mineral as we can observe it without a microscope or other tool is called its habit and may look quite different from the crystal unit inside. Many minerals appear in several habits.

Needlelike
Some crystals are long and thin, resembling groups of needles.

Stalactitic
Stalactitic crystals form as tubes and usually grow in caves (see page 52).

Cubic
Crystals of rock candy are cubes. When many form at the same time, they grow together, with crystals sharing faces and corners.

Radiating
Crystals of this habit fan out from a central point and form spheres.

Grapelike
This blobby habit is formed when fine needles clump together.

Prismatic
The most common crystal habit has long rods with flat ends.

Make your own

You can grow crystals in the same way that they form in nature. Water with chemicals dissolved in it is like the mineral-rich fluids that seep through rocks. As the water evaporates, solid crystals will form.

Luster

The way that a crystal reflects light is called its luster. This is not related to its color—it is more about how shiny or dull its surface is.

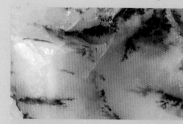

Greasy
A slippery-looking crystal, such as orpiment, can reflect light brightly.

Resinous
This luster gives a crystal a deep gloss. It can look similar to a greasy or glassy luster.

Glassy
This luster is more formally called vitreous. Vitreous surfaces look like glass.

Metallic
Shiny crystals, such as galena and magnetite, look like they are made of metal.

Silky
An opaque mineral with a sometimes-fibrous (fiberlike) surface sheen, such as chrysotile, has a silky luster.

Salt crystals
Make cubic salt crystals by dissolving lots of ordinary table salt in warm water. Crystals will form on a string hanging in the water as the water cools.

Crystal garden
Many chemistry kits include alum salts. These are easy to grow and will quickly turn into a "garden" of branching, brightly colored crystals.

Silicates [All over the world]

Silicates are the most widespread group of minerals. These tough crystals all contain silicon and oxygen. There are over 1,000 different silicates (about one-third of all known minerals), split into families based on the arrangements of their atoms.

Spodumene

Usually ash gray in color, spodumene is most often found as big crystals in pegmatite rock (see page 34). A green form is known as the gem hiddenite; the gem kunzite is pink- to lilac-colored spodumene.

Battery power

Spodumene is rich in lithium, a soft metal that is used in rechargeable batteries.

CELL PHONE BATTERIES

Color	Gray-white, sometimes yellow, green, pink, or lilac
Hardness	6.5–7
Mineral family	Inosilicates

Zircon

This mineral gets its name from the Arabic word meaning "golden" (although it comes in other colors, too). Zircon's small, hard crystals last for billions of years; some date back nearly to our planet's birth.

Dating agent

Shiny zircon crystals glint brightly from igneous rocks. Geologists check the chemicals inside zircons to measure how old the rocks are.

Color	Colorless, brown, gold, red, orange, or green
Hardness	7.5
Mineral family	Nesosilicates

Flashy finisher

Silicate mica, which is present in almost every rock, crumbles into tiny flakes that sparkle when they catch the light. Mica flakes give a glittery, metallic finish to the paint used on cars.

METALLIC-FINISH PAINT

Clay

Tiny grains of silicate minerals, many thousands of times smaller than sand, form clay. When wet, clay can be molded into just about any shape, but once heated, the silicate grains fuse into hard pottery.

90% of rock on Earth is made of silicates

Olivine

Named for its distinctive olive color, this is the most abundant mineral on Earth, although most of it lies buried deep below the surface. Olivine has been detected in meteorites and comets, and also in Moon rocks (see page 59).

Green world

Scientists calculate that half of Earth's upper mantle is made of olivine, in the form of peridotite rock (see page 34).

Color	Olive green
Hardness	6.5–7
Mineral family	Orthosilicates

Terra-cotta warriors

Over 2,200 years ago, the first emperor of China was buried with an army of 8,000 life-size soldiers sculpted from clay.

Color	Gray, yellow, red, or brown
Hardness	2–2.5
Mineral family	Phyllosilicates

Feldspar

Two varieties of this mineral make up over 60 percent of the rock in Earth's crust. Alkali feldspar forms the main crystals in igneous granite (see page 35), metamorphic gneiss (see page 56), and sedimentary sandstone (see page 44). Plagioclase feldspar is a key ingredient of the igneous rock basalt (see page 34).

Color	Blue, brown, or white
Hardness	6–6.5
Mineral family	Tectosilicates

Moonstone
The finest alkali feldspar specimens are called moonstones. Their soft sheen comes from a surface layer of microscopic crystals.

High-tech minerals [Special

Minerals play an increasingly important role in today's cutting-edge industries and technologies. In fact, the more scientists discover about the amazing properties of minerals, the more uses we find for them.

Making stones

Many gemstones, such as rubies, diamonds, sapphires, emeralds, and garnets, can be made in laboratories. Synthetic (artificially made) stones have many uses in industry and engineering. Gem-quality synthetic stones are also used in jewelry.

Synthetic diamonds
Making artificial diamonds requires very high temperatures and mind-blowing pressure. Diamond is the world's hardest material, so many synthetic diamonds are used to make cutting tools.

2,732°F
(1,500°C): the temperature **needed to make** artificial diamonds

Garnet group

Garnets are semiprecious silicate minerals found in many igneous and metamorphic rocks. They are found in a variety of colors, most commonly red. Synthetic garnet crystals are used as gemstones and in lasers.

GARNET

FIRING A LASER AT THE MOON

Shoot for the Moon

Scientists can accurately calculate the distance to the Moon by measuring the time it takes for pulses of light to travel to the Moon and back. They fire a garnet laser at reflectors left on the Moon by astronauts, which bounce the light back to Earth.

Awesome conductors

Copper-containing minerals are used to make special superconducting materials. Superconductors have no electrical resistance, so they are superb conductors of electricity.

AZURITE AND MALACHITE (COPPER-CONTAINING MINERALS)

SUPERCONDUCTING MAGLEV TRAIN

Marvelously magnetic

Passing a large electric current though a superconductor turns the superconductor into a powerful magnet. It can even hover in the air if held up by magnetic forces. Maglev trains use superconducting magnets to float above the tracks.

Sapphire shield

Some computer chips and electronic components incorporate sapphires. These gems are excellent electrical insulators. They are used to shield electronics from sudden, unwanted surges of electrical current.

RUBIES

SAPPHIRE

ZEOLITE

Ruby engineering

High-quality mechanical clocks and watches often contain precious rubies, and sometimes sapphires. These durable gems are used to make pivots for the wheels and cogs of clockwork mechanisms.

Supersponges

Zeolites are silicate minerals that contain aluminum. They are riddled with microscopic pores, so they act like sponges and suck liquids onto their surfaces. This property makes zeolites important in many industrial processes.

ELECTRONIC CIRCUITRY

Silicon on sapphire

Microscopic silicon circuits are deposited onto the surfaces of synthetic sapphires in high-performance electronic chips. Only synthetic sapphire crystals of the highest purity are used.

JEWEL PIVOTS IN CLOCKWORK

Friction beaters

For a clock to keep accurate time, its cogs and wheels must turn with minimal friction—the force that acts between moving parts to slow them down. Ruby pivots are ultratough and supersmooth, so they help keep friction to a minimum.

OIL REFINERY

Cracking minerals

Zeolites are used in oil refineries to help with cracking—the process that splits crude oil into simpler, more useful substances, such as gasoline, diesel, and other fuels. Zeolites are also used in the manufacturing of laundry detergents.

Solid water

Supercool ice tunnels snake beneath the glaciers of Vatnajökull in southern Iceland. These blue caves are formed when Earth's inner heat collides with intense cold at its surface. They are carved out as fast-moving water heated by active volcanoes meets slow, steadily moving glacier ice. Although you rarely see ice listed as a mineral, it actually is one, since it is solid, naturally occurring, and inorganic (not made of living things).

Ore minerals [Making metal]

Geologists are always looking for ores—valuable rocks and minerals containing useful metals. Some metals, such as gold and silver, occur naturally in a pure form, but most metals must be extracted from minerals. In a sulfide ore, the metal is combined with sulfur; in an oxide, it is combined with oxygen.

Stay stainless
The brilliant shine of this juicer is produced by a thin coat of chromium, commonly called chrome plate. Chromium can also be mixed with iron to make shiny, rust-resistant stainless steel.

Scheelite

This mineral, whose crystals form eight-sided double pyramids, is a major ore of the metal tungsten. Scheelite fluoresces, or glows bright blue in ultraviolet light, so miners use UV to locate it underground.

Color	White, brown, or gray
Hardness	4.5–5
Mineral family	Tungstates

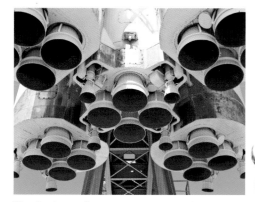

Rocket engines
Tungsten is added to other metals to make rocket engine nozzles, which can withstand the intense heat of blastoff.

Chromite

This is the only ore of the metal chromium, so chromite is a very expensive mineral. Lumps of chromite form in peridotite rocks deep within Earth's mantle.

Color	Metallic
Hardness	5.5
Mineral family	Oxides

Magnetic rocks

Naturally magnetic rocks are called lodestones. They contain the mineral magnetite, which is an iron ore. The first compasses were made from lodestones.

Liquid dancer
A ferro fluid is an oil mixed with tiny particles of magnetite. A strong magnetic field pulls the liquid into strange shapes.

Galena

Used as a source of lead since ancient times, galena is still the main ore of this metal. It is a heavy mineral, because the lead that it contains is very dense. Galena is often found alongside sphalerite deposits.

Color	Dark, metallic gray
Hardness	2.5
Mineral family	Sulfides

Chalcopyrite

Although other minerals contain more copper, chalcopyrite is the most abundant copper ore, making it the major source of this metal. Most of the copper in the world is locked up in rocks with tiny chalcopyrite veins running through them.

Color	Brassy or golden yellow
Hardness	3.5–4
Mineral family	Sulfides

Mining copper
Chalcopyrite is often extracted from large open mines (left), but it is also mined underground.

Lead ore
Galena is the most important of over 60 lead ores. It is easily identified by its cube-shaped crystals and metallic sheen.

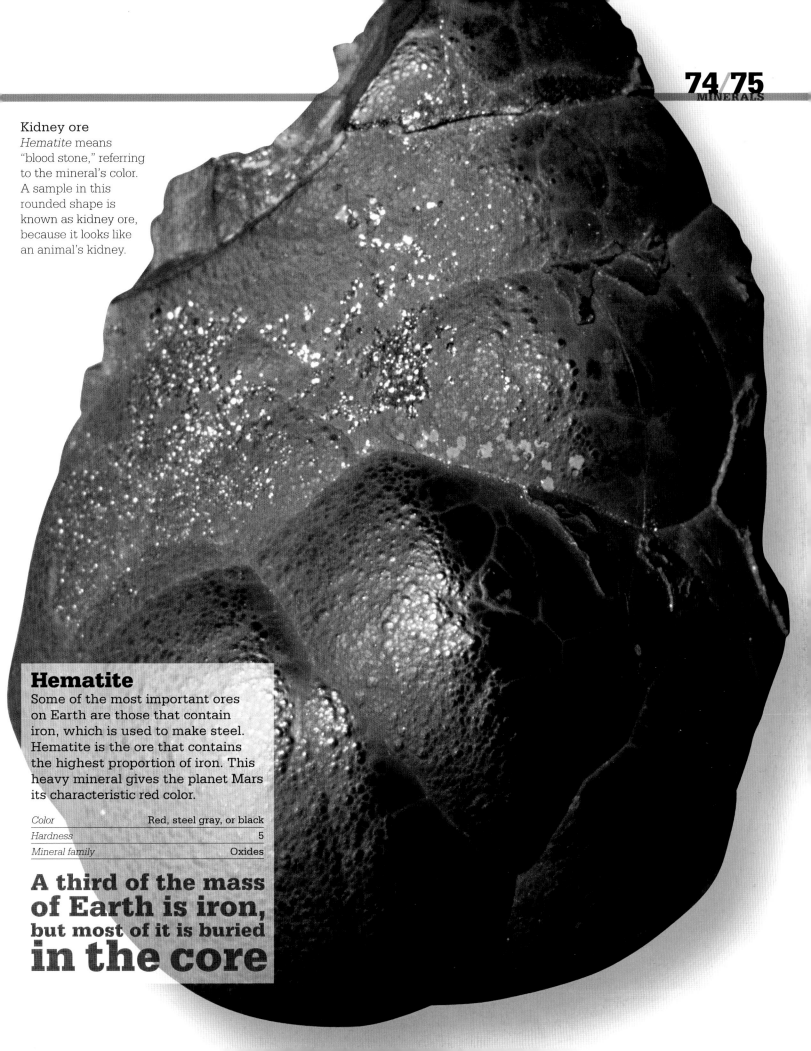

Kidney ore
Hematite means "blood stone," referring to the mineral's color. A sample in this rounded shape is known as kidney ore, because it looks like an animal's kidney.

Hematite

Some of the most important ores on Earth are those that contain iron, which is used to make steel. Hematite is the ore that contains the highest proportion of iron. This heavy mineral gives the planet Mars its characteristic red color.

Color	Red, steel gray, or black
Hardness	5
Mineral family	Oxides

A third of the mass of Earth is iron, but most of it is buried in the core

Precious metals

Gold, silver, and platinum are among the world's most rare and valuable minerals. Known as precious metals, they often occur in their native state, meaning that they are not combined with other elements as ores (see page 74).

Money
Precious metals were ideal for use as coins, because they last a long time without wearing away.

Store of wealth
Although gold and silver coins are no longer used, banks still keep bars of precious metals.

Forever golden
Gold is long lasting because it is unreactive, which means that it does not combine easily with other chemicals. This is how it always keeps its shine and why NASA used gold for the "Golden Record" that it sent into space on the two *Voyager* spacecrafts in 1977.

Interstellar message
The *Voyager*s are each carrying a gold-plated record of messages from Earth. Each record's case has diagrams that show how to play the video portion of the recording (right).

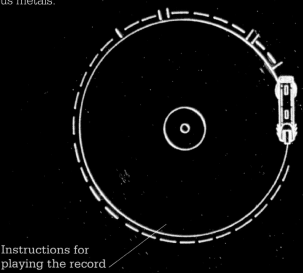

Instructions for playing the record

A side view of the Golden Record

Golden light
When tiny flakes of gold are mixed into glass, they play tricks with light. Depending on their size, they produce red, orange, and even blue colors— an effect used in stained glass windows.

The Lycurgus Cup
The color-changing glass in this ornate Roman cup from the fourth century CE contains specks of gold and silver.

Color change
The green glass turns red and pink when light shines through it.

A diagram showing Earth's location in the galaxy, with directions and distances to 14 prominent pulsar stars (stars that emit pulses of radio waves)

Seeking gold

Centuries ago, experimenters called alchemists searched for the philosopher's stone—a legendary substance that they believed could turn ordinary metals, such as lead, into precious gold. Had the alchemists succeeded, gold would have become very common and lost much of its value!

Unwanted discovery

In 1669, alchemist Hennig Brand was looking for the philosopher's stone when he accidentally discovered a glowing new element, phosphorus.

A *Voyager* record's gold-plated aluminum case

A diagram of the video signals on the recording

Instructions for decoding the images on the Golden Record

A circle—the first image on the record, when it is correctly decoded

The key to understanding all the diagrams on the case, based on the hydrogen atom

1.34%: the percentage of an Olympic gold medal that is gold

Silver

As well as being a precious metal and valuable for coinage, silver has many practical uses. It is a great conductor of electricity and a superb reflector of light, and it is also excellent at killing bacteria.

Water for astronauts

Astronauts on the International Space Station use silver to purify water recycled from their sweat and urine!

One by one

In the future, we will build electronic components atom by atom. Each spike is one atom.

Noble metal

Platinum is even less reactive than gold is. It is described as a noble metal, because it rarely combines with more common elements.

Building with atoms

Scientists use microscopic platinum probes to pick up atoms and build them into structures.

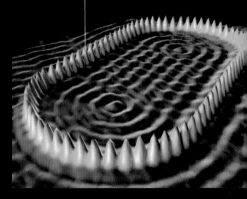

Mining [Digging deep]

Valuable raw materials, such as metal ores, coal, salt, and clays, lie buried underground, mixed with mountains of soil. Digging such resources out of the ground is a big—and dirty—business.

Ancient mines
The earliest mines were dug to extract clays, and stone such as flint. Early people used flint to make tools like axes.

Open pit mine
Deep inside the Bingham Canyon Mine in Utah, explosives are used to blast chunks of copper ore out of the ground. This mine is the largest artificially made hole in the world.

Copper conveyor
From the crushing plant, a 5-mile-long (8 km) series of conveyor belts carries the crushed copper ore out of the mine to the processing and refining area.

Grimes graves
This Neolithic flint mine in Norfolk, UK, has around 400 mining pits. The pits were dug about 5,000 years ago.

A big, big, big hole!
The Bingham mine plunges down over half a mile (1 km) and is 2.75 miles (4.4 km) across—that's like 38 soccer fields laid end to end!

Milestones
Many ancient cultures mined stones for building and gems for their beauty. When people discovered that they could extract tough metals from rocks, metal ores were dug up and refined.

1330 BCE

Ancient Egyptian gold
The Egyptians mined gems (such as lapis lazuli) and gold to make sacred ornaments.

100 BCE

Stone aqueduct
Roman engineers were able to build strong structures with stones excavated from quarries.

1300 CE

Making steel
The demand for steel armor and weapons led to a surge in iron mining in the Middle Ages.

Mining perils

Mining is risky work—not only for miners using explosives or digging underground, but also for the environment. It leaves unsightly scars on the land, and the refining methods used to free metals from their ores can pollute plant and animal habitats.

River pollution
Acid leaking from old copper mines has polluted this river in Australia, killing rainforest trees.

Safety lamp
The Davy lamp, invented in 1815, was a safety lamp used by coal miners. The oil flame inside did not ignite any explosive gases that leaked into mines.

More here
For key to symbols, see page 112.

coal mine copper refining
Davy lamp **gold rush**
Industrial Revolution
open pit mine

You Wouldn't Want to Be a 19th-Century Coal Miner in England! by John Malam

Paint Your Wagon (1969) is a musical about the California gold rush, starring Clint Eastwood.

Visit the **Lackawanna Coal Mine** for a tour of a restored historic mine in Scranton, PA.

The visitor center at the **Bingham Canyon Mine**, UT (also known as Kennecott Visitors Center), features hands-on exhibits.

At the **Big Pit: National Coal Museum**, in Blaenafon, UK, you can ride an elevator 295 feet (90 m) down an old mine shaft and learn about life in the mine.

Never go into a mine without a guide.

1830 — Engine power
Coal mines provided fuel for the steam engines that powered the Industrial Revolution.

1849 — Gold rush
Discoveries of precious metals sparked gold rushes in the US, Canada, and Australia.

2010 — Chilean miners saved
In 2010, 33 copper miners were rescued after being trapped 2,300 ft (700 m) underground.

Carbonates and others

Carbonates, borates, and nitrates are important minerals in Earth's crust, but most are soft and easily broken down by wind and rain. Borates and nitrates are uncommon, but carbonates are more plentiful, and some contain useful metals.

Magnesite

This carbonate mineral is one of the most important ores (see page 74) of magnesium, a light yet strong metal that is used in aircraft, cars, and bikes. Veins of magnesite crystals form in limestone when hot, mineral-rich water is forced through holes in the rock.

Party time!
Magnesium metal burns with a brilliant light, which is why it is used in fireworks, including holiday sparklers.

Color	White, gray, or yellow-brown
Hardness	3.5–4
Mineral family	Carbonates

Malachite

One of the most beautiful minerals, malachite is a copper ore. Malachite was probably the first ore from which copper was extracted by smelting, or heating the ore with charcoal in a furnace, around 7,000 years ago.

Color	Green
Hardness	3.5–4
Mineral family	Carbonates

Green swirls
Malachite is named after mallow, a plant with bright green leaves. Polishing the mineral shows off its banded patterns.

Rhodochrosite

The rose pink or bloodred crystals of this carbonate can be spectacular. The Inca people of Peru believed that rhodochrosite was the blood of their dead rulers, so rhodochrosite is sometimes called the Inca rose. The color comes from manganese in the crystals.

Color	Rose pink to red
Hardness	3.5–4
Mineral family	Carbonates

Striking beauty
Rhodochrosite chips easily. Therefore, its crystals, although very beautiful, are rarely used in jewelry.

Borax

This borate mineral is an ingredient in strong soaps and cosmetics. Borax is also an important source of the element boron, used to make bulletproof vests and the protective heat shields on spacecraft.

Color	White
Hardness	2–2.5
Mineral family	Borates

Cotton ball
Borax is left behind when seasonal lakes evaporate during the summer. Fist-size "cotton balls" made of borax fibers sometimes form on these dried-up lake beds.

Rocket powder

Nitrate chemicals are used to make solid rocket fuels, explosives, and fertilizers. Nitratine is a naturally occurring nitrate. It absorbs water easily and readily dissolves, so it is found only in deserts and dry caves.

Into orbit
The side boosters of this Ariane 5 rocket, which thrust the spacecraft into the air, are powered by fuel-containing nitrates.

Calcite

Calcite, also called calcium carbonate, is the main ingredient of limestone, chalk, and marble. Calcite dissolves easily in water. Aquatic creatures extract calcite from the water and use it to build their shells. Ocean reefs, such as Australia's Great Barrier Reef, are made entirely from the calcite skeletons of coral polyps.

Color	White or colorless
Hardness	3
Mineral family	Carbonates

When struck in the dark, calcite emits light

Double vision

Iceland spar is a transparent variety of calcite. A light ray traveling through an Iceland spar crystal splits in two, producing double images of objects behind the crystal.

Many forms

Calcite crystals grow in more than 300 different shapes. Nailhead spar is a type of calcite with flat-topped crystals that resemble the heads of nails.

Common salt

Salt has been mined and traded for thousands of years. Here, workers in Ethiopia, Africa, cut slabs of salt from a desert salt flat; the blocks will next be loaded onto camel caravans. Most salt deposits occur as thick layers that were left behind when ancient seas and salty lakes evaporated. Salt is a useful mineral: It flavors and preserves food, it is spread on roads in winter to prevent ice from forming, and small amounts of it are essential for good health.

Sulfates and phosphates

Sulfates contain sulfur and oxygen, and many of them are useful ores (see page 74). Phosphates contain phosphorus and oxygen. Living things need phosphates to function healthily. Most of the phosphate mined is used to make plant fertilizers.

Sphalerite

This zinc mineral contains sulfur but no oxygen, making it a sulfide. It is the principal ore of zinc. This metal is used in batteries and is coated onto iron and steel objects to protect them from rusting.

Zinc ore
To produce zinc metal, these crystals must be crushed and roasted, then burned.

Color	Brown, black, or yellow
Hardness	3.5–4
Mineral family	Sulfides

Turquoise

Beautiful blue-green turquoise was one of the first gemstones mined. Ancient Egyptian, Persian, Native American, and Chinese cultures all used it for decorative purposes.

Color	Blue-green
Hardness	2.6–2.8
Mineral family	Phosphates

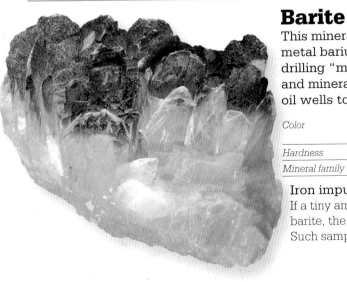

Aztec mask
For the Aztec people of Mexico, turquoise was an important stone. They decorated sacred objects with tiny turquoise tiles.

Fluorescent minerals

Turquoise and many other minerals fluoresce—they glow when viewed in ultraviolet (UV) light. Fluorite, for which this quality is named, is the best example. Fluorite glows blue in UV, while turquoise glows green.

FLUORITE IN NORMAL LIGHT

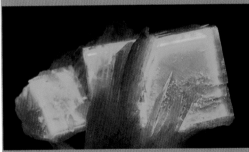

FLUORITE IN UV LIGHT

Apatite

Apatite crystals tend to be small, but they are very common in rocks. High-quality crystals are sometimes used as gemstones. Plants obtain phosphates from naturally occurring apatite in the soil or from fertilizers.

Color	Green, yellowish, brown, or purple
Hardness	5
Mineral family	Phosphates

Barite

This mineral is the main source of the metal barium. Barite is used to make drilling "mud"—a mixture of water and mineral powder that is piped into oil wells to help drills run smoothly.

Color	Colorless or white, often tinged with red or banded
Hardness	3–3.5
Mineral family	Sulfates

Iron impurities
If a tiny amount of iron is present in barite, the mineral crystals appear red. Such samples are called rose rocks.

Tooth enamel
Apatite is the one of the few minerals that living things can produce. It is the hard material in tooth enamel and bone.

Ram's horn gypsum
Gypsum crystals are found in many different shapes. When one side of a crystal grows faster than the other, it can produce a shape like a ram's horn.

Gypsum

Crystals of this soft mineral may be left behind as salt water evaporates (see page 49). Gypsum occurs on the sites of ancient salt pans and seabeds, and also in caves. One cave in Mexico contains gypsum crystals up to 33 feet (10 m) long.

Color	White, colorless, or gray, occasionally yellowish
Hardness	2
Mineral family	Sulfates

Not all minerals are useful or beautiful. Many contain toxic substances that can cause mental problems, sickness, or even death. These poisonous minerals can wreak havoc if they are used in everyday materials or if they find their way into the water supply.

Radon gas emitted by radium-containing minerals underground can make houses radioactive

Hellish breath

The Hydra is a mythical beast with breath so foul it can kill a human. It is said to live in springs inside volcanic caves. Such caves really are full of toxic fumes—but they come from volcanic activity underground, not monsters!

GREEK HERO HERACLES KILLING THE HYDRA

Know your poison

People are often unaware of the dangers that minerals can pose. Some toxic minerals dissolve, poisoning wells and drinking water. Others produce lethal radioactivity or have fibers that can enter and irritate the lungs.

Death from lead

The Roman emperor Nero, who supposedly played a fiddle while watching Rome burn, was said to be insane. His madness may have been due to lead poisoning, caused by the lead pots in which the syrup that sweetened his wine was cooked.

GALENA, A LEAD ORE USED BY THE ROMANS

NERO AMID THE RUINS OF ROME (64 CE)

Arsenic peril

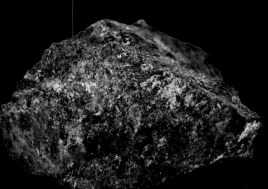

Long-term exposure to the element arsenic causes a range of potentially fatal illnesses. In Bangladesh, well water is often contaminated with arsenic from underground deposits of minerals such as arsenopyrite.

ARSENOPYRITE, AN IRON
ARSENIC SULFIDE

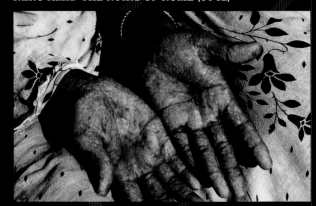

DISEASE CAUSED BY ARSENIC, BANGLADESH

Maddening cinnabar

The saying "mad as a hatter" refers to an illness suffered by hatmakers in the 18th and 19th centuries. Mercury, extracted from the mineral cinnabar, was used in felt hats. It caused brain damage in many hatters, which other people mistook for insanity.

CINNABAR, ALSO KNOWN AS RED MERCURY

MAD HATTER (*ALICE'S ADVENTURES IN WONDERLAND*)

Radioactive pitchblende

The most dangerous ore of all is pitchblende. It contains the deadly radioactive elements uranium, radium, thorium, and polonium. The mineral uraninite is extracted from pitchblende and refined to provide uranium for nuclear bombs and power plants.

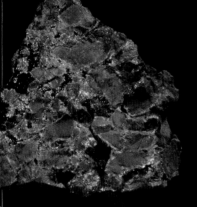

PITCHBLENDE, A PRIMARY MINERAL ORE OF URANIUM

NUCLEAR EXPLOSION

Asbestos alarm

Asbestos is a general name for minerals that grow as very thin fibers. Asbestos resists burning, so it was used as a building material and in fireproof curtains. It is now banned in many countries, because its fine fibers can cause fatal lung cancers.

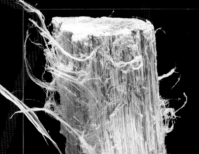

CHRYSOTILE, OR WHITE ASBESTOS

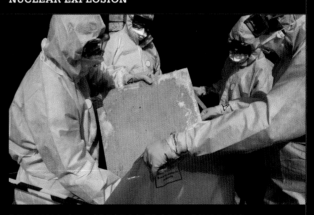

REMOVAL OF ASBESTOS FROM A BUILDING

Death of Napoleon

While a prisoner on the island of Saint Helena, French emperor Napoleon Bonaparte lived in rooms decorated with bright green wallpaper. He may have been poisoned by arsenic in the orpiment and copper minerals that gave the paper its color.

In 1961, scientists analyzing samples of Napoleon's hair reported that it contained a high level of arsenic

Earthquakes [Bad vibes]

The rocks of Earth's crust feel solid and immovable, but they are actually constantly in motion. Forces deep within the planet slowly push vast chunks of the crust over the surface, sometimes shaking the ground—with devastating results.

What is an earthquake?

An earthquake is a sudden release of energy that travels through the ground as deep rumbles of sound, mostly too low to hear. The rumbles are called seismic waves. It's a bit like when you feel the ground vibrate as a car with a loud stereo passes by—except that with an earthquake, the vibrations are far more powerful.

Tsunami

Undersea quakes create huge tsunami waves as the rocking seabed sloshes the water above it around. Tsunamis rise to terrifying heights as they approach land.

How quakes happen

The rocks inside Earth are churning around like water boiling in very slow motion. This movement pushes slabs of crust across Earth's surface. The slabs often get stuck as they grind past one another. Forces build up until—*snap!*—the rocks break free. It's a quake!

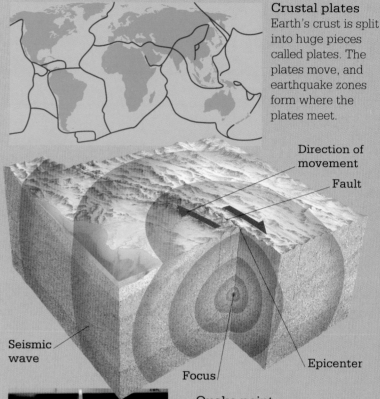

Crustal plates

Earth's crust is split into huge pieces called plates. The plates move, and earthquake zones form where the plates meet.

Direction of movement

Fault

Seismic wave

Focus

Epicenter

SEISMIC WAVE DETECTOR

Quake point

An earthquake starts at a focus point underground. Seismic shock waves travel out from the focus, causing the ground at the surface to shake. The point on the surface directly above the focus is called the epicenter.

California quake

Quakes happen every year, but some are truly catastrophic. At 5:12 AM on April 18, 1906, a violent quake hit San Francisco, CA. Shifting rocks along the San Andreas Fault—the boundary between two crustal plates—shattered the great city.

Quake-caused fire
Gas pipelines were broken in the quake, and fires broke out soon after. The fires raged out of control for three days.

Devastation
The earthquake lasted only about 65 seconds but left the city in ruins. Nearly 500 city blocks were destroyed.

Cracked up
The earthquake created a crack in the ground that was 296 miles (476 km) long.

City in ruins
The San Francisco quake killed around 3,000 people. Three out of every four San Francisco citizens were left without homes.

More here
For key to symbols, see page 112.

EARTHQUAKE RECORDS

Largest US earthquake: A 9.2 magnitude quake hit Prince William Sound, AK, on March 28, 1964.

Largest recorded earthquake: A quake measuring a massive 9.5 on the Richter scale—more than ten times stronger than the San Francisco quake of 1906—hit Chile on May 22, 1960.

fault plate boundaries
primary waves
secondary waves
shadow zone
tectonic plate
San Andreas Fault
Richter scale
Tohoku earthquake and tsunami

Earthquake Exhibit: Life on a Dynamic Planet is a major new Earth science feature at the California Academy of Sciences, San Francisco, CA.

The Great Hanshin-Awaji Earthquake Memorial commemorates the disastrous tremor that hit the Japanese city of Kobe in 1995.

Glorious
ge

* What makes diamonds sparkle?

* What is a privateer?

* Which gem turns yellow when it is heated?

Sparkling stones

Of the 3,000 or so minerals on Earth, only about 130 form gems. Many of these sparkling, breathtakingly beautiful stones can be cut into exquisite shapes and polished so that they seem to shine with internal light. On the next four pages, you can see cut or polished gems alongside their naturally occurring forms.

GARNET

AMBER

OPAL

SPINEL

LAPIS LAZULI

DIAMOND

JADE

AMETHYST

TOPAZ

TIGEREYE

LABRADORITE

SAPPHIRE

EMERALD

RUBY

JET

SODALITE

TANZANITE

PEARL

MALACHITE

ZIRCON

DIOPTASE

ROSE QUARTZ

MORGANITE

CHRYSOCOLLA

HEMATITE

AQUAMARINE

SUGILITE

CARNELIAN

RHODOCHROSITE

JASPER

PERIDOT

TURQUOISE

VARISCITE

AGATE

TOURMALINE

CORAL

Cut stones [Jewels

Symbols of status and wealth, gems have long been treasured by the rich and powerful. But the perfect gems in jewelry all started out as rough, mined minerals. They had to be shaped by skilled craftspeople into the shimmering stones you see in shops and museums.

Saint Edward's sapphire
This lovely sapphire was taken from the ring of the English king Edward the Confessor. It could date from the year 1042.

Elizabeth I's pearls
Unlike the other stones on the crown, these big pearls are made by living things—oysters.

Crowning glory

The Imperial State Crown is part of the crown jewels of the United Kingdom. It includes exquisite examples of the five major gemstones: diamonds, emeralds, rubies, sapphires, and pearls. Large gemstones are so valuable that they have often belonged to kings and queens—and have been stolen and fought over.

Gems in the Imperial State Crown of Great Britain:

2,868

diamonds, 17 sapphires, 11 emeralds, and 269 pearls

Source of the sparkle

Gleaming and glittering, jewels play games with light, catching and throwing it around a room. Their characteristic colorful sparkle is produced as the minerals reflect and transmit the light rays that pass through them.

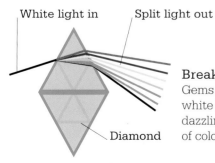

White light in

Split light out

Diamond

Breaking up light
Gems split ordinary white light into a dazzling spectrum of colors.

in the crown]

Color

An important quality of a jewel is its color. This depends largely on the type of atoms in the stone and the way that they are arranged. Impurities also affect color. For example, impurities in the mineral corundum can create two different gems: rubies and sapphires. The rarer the color, the more valuable the jewel.

Ruby
Red corundum is called ruby. The color is produced by chromium impurities.

Sapphire
When corundum has iron and copper impurities, it becomes a blue sapphire.

Turquoise
Opaque gems like turquoise (whose color is due to its chemical makeup) can also have very intense colors.

Shaping gems

Cutting a gemstone usually creates facets. These flat faces make the gem flash and sparkle. Different cuts, such as those below, have been developed to enhance the beauty of gems and increase their value.

ROUND **PRINCESS** **OCTAGON** **RADIANT**

MARQUISE **HEART** **PEAR** **TRILLIANT**

ASSCHER **OVAL** **TRIANGLE** **CUSHION**

Head ornament
The British monarch wears the Imperial State Crown only once a year.

Fleurs-de-lis
These diamond-encrusted flowers have central rubies.

Black Prince's ruby
This old stone is not actually a ruby at all. It is a spinel—the world's largest uncut specimen.

Cullinan II
This diamond was cut from the largest gem-quality diamond ever found, discovered in South Africa in 1905.

More here

For key to symbols, see page 112.

brilliants inclusion four Cs **corundum** **carat** crown jewels Cullinan diamond

The Pink Panther (1963) is a comedy caper about a bumbling detective on the trail of a jewel thief. It was also remade in 2006.

Diamonds Are Forever (1971) is the seventh James Bond movie, in which Bond infiltrates a diamond-smuggling ring.

The British crown jewels are held at the **Tower of London**, UK. Check out the Beefeater guards, too!

The Big Hole, in Kimberley, South Africa, is an old diamond mine run by the De Beers company.

Visit the **Diamond Museum Amsterdam**, in the Netherlands, to see a diamond's journey from raw mineral to jewel.

Try the traditional Myanmar (Burmese) method of distinguishing true rubies and sapphires. Touch them with your tongue—they feel like ice!

Treasure hunters [Plunder

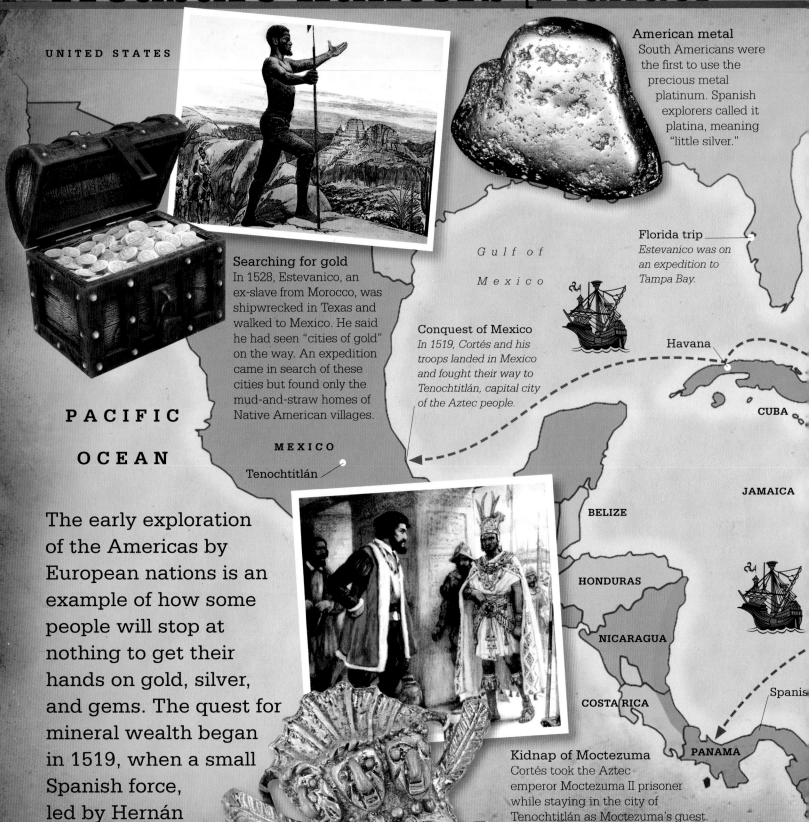

UNITED STATES

American metal
South Americans were the first to use the precious metal platinum. Spanish explorers called it platina, meaning "little silver."

Florida trip
Estevanico was on an expedition to Tampa Bay.

Gulf of Mexico

Havana

CUBA

JAMAICA

BELIZE

HONDURAS

NICARAGUA

COSTA RICA

PANAMA

Spanis

Searching for gold
In 1528, Estevanico, an ex-slave from Morocco, was shipwrecked in Texas and walked to Mexico. He said he had seen "cities of gold" on the way. An expedition came in search of these cities but found only the mud-and-straw homes of Native American villages.

Conquest of Mexico
In 1519, Cortés and his troops landed in Mexico and fought their way to Tenochtitlán, capital city of the Aztec people.

PACIFIC OCEAN

MEXICO

Tenochtitlán

The early exploration of the Americas by European nations is an example of how some people will stop at nothing to get their hands on gold, silver, and gems. The quest for mineral wealth began in 1519, when a small Spanish force, led by Hernán Cortés, invaded Aztec Mexico.

SILVER MASK FROM MEXICO

Kidnap of Moctezuma
Cortés took the Aztec emperor Moctezuma II prisoner while staying in the city of Tenochtitlán as Moctezuma's guest. The Spanish invaders demanded a huge ransom from the Aztec people for the release of their emperor— enough to fill entire rooms with gold, silver, and jewels!

High-seas robbery

The Spanish carried their bounty of gold, emeralds, and other treasures back to Spain in large ships called galleons. Other European countries decided to steal it and employed pirates, known as privateers, to attack the slow-moving treasure ships.

Treasure fleet
For the journeys between Seville, in Spain, and the Americas, Spanish galleons traveled in heavily armed convoys called flotas.

Privateers attack
From the 1660s to the 1730s, English, Dutch, and French pirates preyed on Spanish fleets as they set out from Caribbean ports for the long journey across the Atlantic Ocean.

Caribbean wrecks
The remains of galleons litter the floor of the Caribbean Sea. Divers explore the wrecks to learn more about the time—and there's always a chance of finding some treasure!

Pieces of eight
These silver coins were known as pieces of eight, because they were worth eight Spanish reales. Gold doubloons were worth four times as much.

HISPANIOLA   Santo Dominigo

Spanish territories (shown in orange)
Treasure from the mainland, called the Spanish Main, was taken to the Caribbean islands, especially Cuba and Hispaniola. There, the treasure ships were prepared for the voyage back to Spain.

ATLANTIC

OCEAN

El dorado, "the golden one"
Explorers mistakenly thought that a city of gold existed in South America. The rumor may have started from a ritual on Lake Guatavita, Colombia, where a chief coated in gold dust—*El dorado*—threw offerings, such as this golden raft, into the lake.

VENEZUELA

GUYANA

Lake Guatavita

COLOMBIA

SOUTH AMERICA

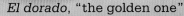

Gemstones

The most colorful, unusual, and eye-catching stones are called gemstones, or gems. These flashy minerals form oversize crystals—with price tags to match. They are often very hard, which means that they don't scratch or lose their shine.

Eye of the tiger
When tigereye is polished, its fibrous crystals give it a silky sheen.

Tigereye

This dusky quartz mineral has a soft shine and smooth gold-colored bands. The bands are made of tiny fibers of silica that fill cracks in the larger crystal. Tigereye is beautiful, but it is not especially rare, so it is called a semiprecious stone. A blue type is known as hawk's eye.

Color	Honey colored to deep brown
Hardness	7
Mineral family	Silicates

Opal

Pearly opal is hardened silica ooze, which occurs as nodules and veins in rocks. Internally, opal is made up of regularly arranged microscopic spheres of silica. These reflect light and create a shimmering effect. The most valuable opals are black.

Color	Colorless, white, yellow, orange, rose red, black, or dark blue
Hardness	5–6
Mineral family	Silicates

Swirling colors
Most opal is dull yellow or red, but gem-quality stones show more colors.

Amethyst

Iron impurities in quartz produce amethyst's purple color. Associated with purity, the gem has a long history—ancient Greeks carved fine cups from it. Amethysts were also used as crown jewels (see pages 96–97). Heating an amethyst turns it into citrine, a yellow stone.

Color	Pale mauve to violet
Hardness	7
Mineral family	Silicates

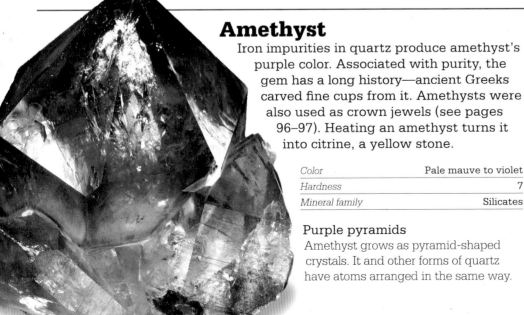

Purple pyramids
Amethyst grows as pyramid-shaped crystals. It and other forms of quartz have atoms arranged in the same way.

Big bling

The core of BPM 37093, a white dwarf star in the constellation Centaurus, is a diamond 2,450 miles (4,000 km) across. It is the largest known crystal in the Universe. Lying 50 light-years away, the star twinkles with 10 billion trillion trillion carats.

BPM 37093, A VARIABLE WHITE DWARF STAR

Diamond may make up one-tenth of the planet Neptune

Jade

Glossy green jade is a favorite stone for carving. Most stone known as jade is made of the silicate mineral nephrite. Another silicate, jadeite, is also called jade, but it is more rare.

Carved dragon
The ancient Chinese believed that jade had sacred qualities and contained cosmic energy. Ornately carved jade figurines are still produced in China today.

Color	Cream to dark green
Hardness	6.5
Mineral family	Silicates

Ruby
Superhard rubies are a gemstone variety of the mineral corundum. They are always bloodred in color. Corundum also forms sapphire. Rubies, sapphires, diamonds, and emeralds are called precious stones, valued for their beauty and rarity.

Color	Red
Hardness	9
Mineral family	Oxide minerals

Gem cutting
Almost as important as a gem's purity and color is the way it is cut. Transparent gemstones, such as rubies, are cut with dozens of flat, angled faces. These bounce light around the inside of the gem and give it an internal fire, or sparkle.

Rock ID kit [What is it?]

Discover more about rocks! Use this quick and easy-to-follow diagram to find out if a rock is igneous, sedimentary, or metamorphic.

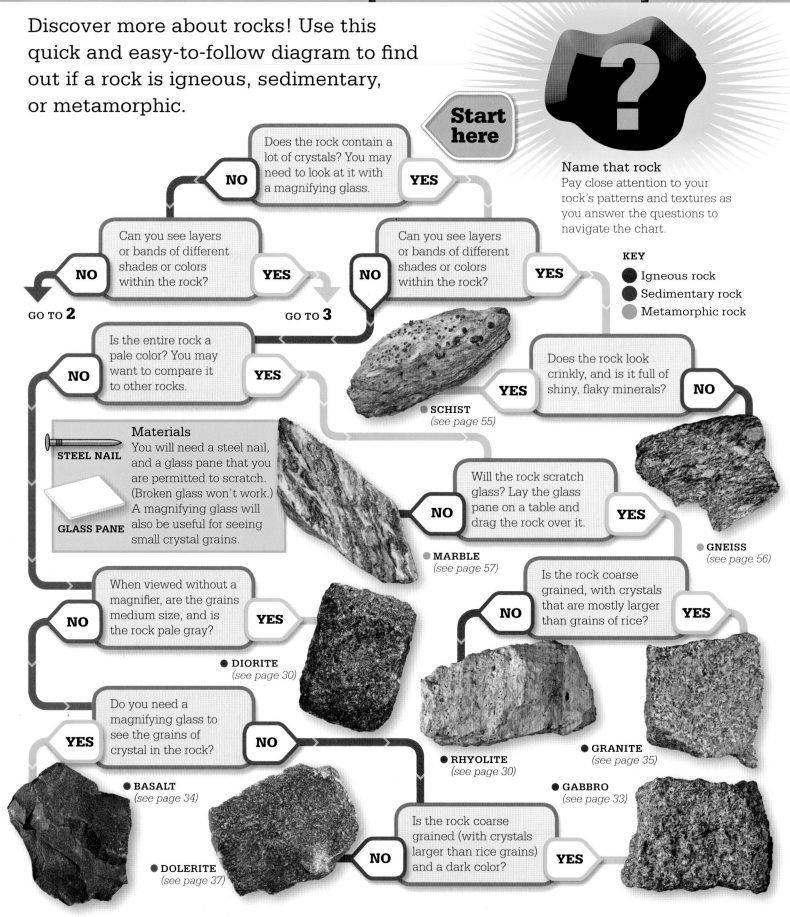

Start here

Name that rock
Pay close attention to your rock's patterns and textures as you answer the questions to navigate the chart.

KEY
● Igneous rock
● Sedimentary rock
● Metamorphic rock

Does the rock contain a lot of crystals? You may need to look at it with a magnifying glass.

NO **YES**

Can you see layers or bands of different shades or colors within the rock?

NO **YES**

GO TO **2**

Can you see layers or bands of different shades or colors within the rock?

NO **YES**

GO TO **3**

Is the entire rock a pale color? You may want to compare it to other rocks.

NO **YES**

Does the rock look crinkly, and is it full of shiny, flaky minerals?

YES **NO**

● SCHIST
(see page 55)

Materials
You will need a steel nail, and a glass pane that you are permitted to scratch. (Broken glass won't work.) A magnifying glass will also be useful for seeing small crystal grains.

STEEL NAIL

GLASS PANE

Will the rock scratch glass? Lay the glass pane on a table and drag the rock over it.

NO **YES**

● MARBLE
(see page 57)

● GNEISS
(see page 56)

Is the rock coarse grained, with crystals that are mostly larger than grains of rice?

NO **YES**

When viewed without a magnifier, are the grains medium size, and is the rock pale gray?

NO **YES**

● DIORITE
(see page 30)

Do you need a magnifying glass to see the grains of crystal in the rock?

YES **NO**

● BASALT
(see page 34)

● RHYOLITE
(see page 30)

● GRANITE
(see page 35)

● GABBRO
(see page 33)

● DOLERITE
(see page 37)

Is the rock coarse grained (with crystals larger than rice grains) and a dark color?

NO **YES**

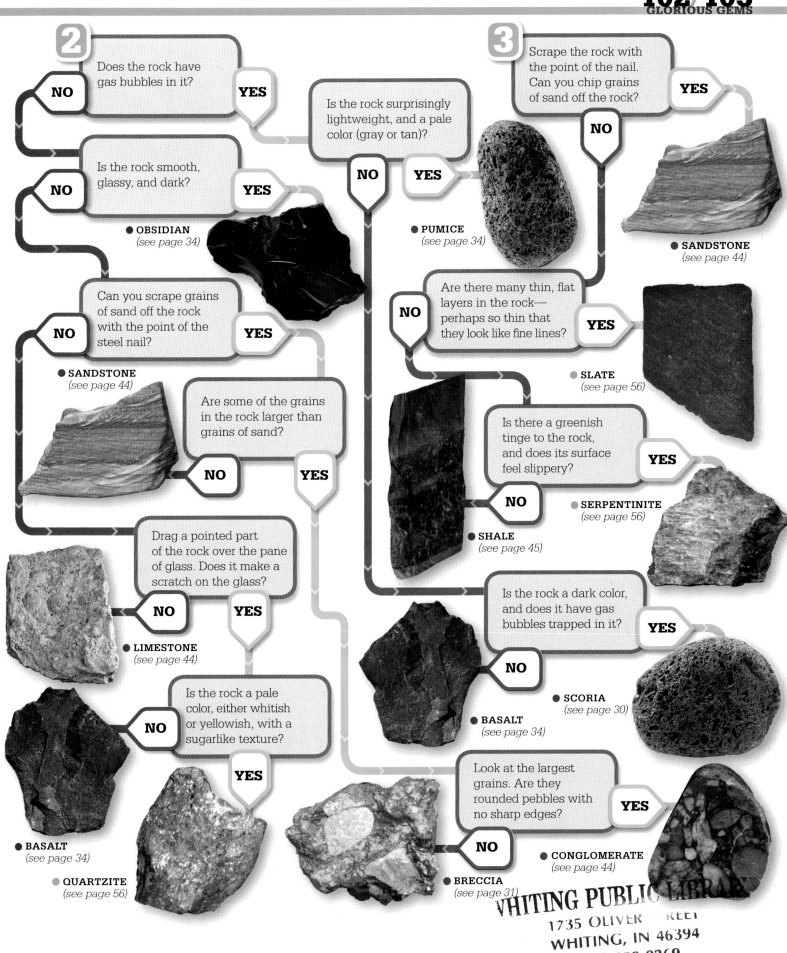

2

Does the rock have gas bubbles in it?

NO

YES

Is the rock smooth, glassy, and dark?

NO

YES

● **OBSIDIAN**
(see page 34)

Is the rock surprisingly lightweight, and a pale color (gray or tan)?

NO

YES

● **PUMICE**
(see page 34)

3

Scrape the rock with the point of the nail. Can you chip grains of sand off the rock?

YES

NO

● **SANDSTONE**
(see page 44)

Can you scrape grains of sand off the rock with the point of the steel nail?

NO

YES

● **SANDSTONE**
(see page 44)

Are some of the grains in the rock larger than grains of sand?

NO

YES

Are there many thin, flat layers in the rock—perhaps so thin that they look like fine lines?

NO

YES

● **SLATE**
(see page 56)

Is there a greenish tinge to the rock, and does its surface feel slippery?

YES

NO

● **SERPENTINITE**
(see page 56)

● **SHALE**
(see page 45)

Drag a pointed part of the rock over the pane of glass. Does it make a scratch on the glass?

NO

YES

● **LIMESTONE**
(see page 44)

Is the rock a pale color, either whitish or yellowish, with a sugarlike texture?

NO

YES

Is the rock a dark color, and does it have gas bubbles trapped in it?

YES

NO

● **SCORIA**
(see page 30)

● **BASALT**
(see page 34)

● **BASALT**
(see page 34)

● **QUARTZITE**
(see page 56)

Look at the largest grains. Are they rounded pebbles with no sharp edges?

YES

NO

● **CONGLOMERATE**
(see page 44)

● **BRECCIA**
(see page 31)

algae
Simple, nonflowering plants that convert sunlight into food but do not have roots, stems, leaves, or other more complex plant structures. Many algae are single-celled organisms. Algae were responsible for first adding oxygen to Earth's atmosphere.

ammonite
An extinct sea creature with a spiral shell. It was distantly related to squids and octopuses, and died out with the dinosaurs 65 million years ago.

amphibian
A cold-blooded animal that lays its eggs in water. The young live in water and breathe through gills; adults live on land and breathe air. Frogs, toads, newts, and salamanders are amphibians.

atom
The basic part of an element. Crystals are made up of repeating units of atoms, arranged in regular patterns. Atoms are composed of smaller particles: electrons, protons, and neutrons.

batholith
An enormous volume of usually coarse- to medium-grained igneous rock that is formed when magma intrudes, or pushes its way, into a large space underground. Batholiths are often rounded but can be any shape.

borate mineral
One of a class of minerals that contain boron bonded tightly to oxygen. Borax is a borate evaporite.

breccia
A sedimentary rock made up of sharp, angular, and irregularly shaped rock fragments.

brilliant
A gemstone, often a diamond, cut in the shape of a cone. A brilliant has many faces, to maximize the amount of light reflected through the top of the gem and thus its sparkle.

butte
A small, isolated hill with a flat top. Larger buttes are also known as mesas or table mountains.

carat
A unit of measurement of the weight of precious stones. A carat is equal to 0.007 ounces (200 mg).

carbonate mineral
One of an important class of rock-forming minerals. A carbonate mineral contains a carbonate group made of carbon bonded tightly to oxygen. Calcite and malachite are carbonates.

cement
A binding material that hardens and, like glue, sticks other materials together. It is made of a base of powdery lime and clay. Cement can also refer to the material that glues grains together in a sedimentary rock.

column
A tall, narrow structure. Basalt lava flows often crack as they cool, forming vertical columns within the rock.

compound
A substance formed by the chemical combination of two or more elements.

conductor
A material that transmits heat or electricity well.

conglomerate
A sedimentary rock made up of rounded and regularly shaped rock fragments.

continent
One of the main landmasses of Earth. Continental crust is generally thicker and lighter than oceanic crust is.

coarse grained
Having large grains or crystals.

core
The center of a planet. Earth's core is composed of an outer core (a layer of liquid iron and nickel) surrounding an inner core (an extremely hot ball of solid iron and nickel).

crust
The top layer of Earth, made of solid rock. The crust under the oceans is 4.5 miles (7 km) thick and mainly basalt; the crust of landmasses, often granite, can be ten times thicker.

crystal
A solid substance with a regular pattern of faces. This shape is due to an orderly arrangement of atoms.

crystallize
To form crystals, often due to the evaporation of water from minerals or to a change in temperature.

cut
The form in which a rough gemstone is shaped to best display its sparkle and fire.

density
The measurement of how much matter is packed into a substance. A quantity of a dense material will weigh more than the same volume of a less dense material.

diatomaceous earth
A soft, naturally occurring sedimentary rock that crumbles easily into powder. Composed of the remains of microscopic creatures called diatoms, this powder is used in toothpaste, as filler material in plastics and rubber, in cat litter, and as a stabilizing agent in dynamite.

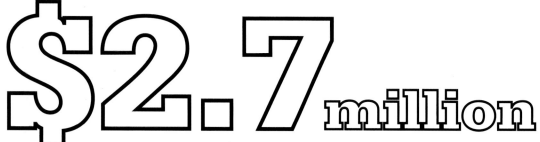

Red diamonds are so rare that in 2007 one sold for **$2.7** million

Glossary

dike
A vertical intrusion of magma that hardens to form igneous rock and cuts across layers of other rock.

dissolve
To mix one substance into another so completely that it is not possible to see the first substance in the second. Solids and gases normally dissolve in liquids. The dissolved mixture is called a solution.

element
A substance that cannot be broken down into simpler ingredients.

epicenter
The point on the surface of the ground directly above the focus of an earthquake.

eruption
The outpouring of liquid lava from a volcano or other opening in the ground.

evaporate
To turn from a liquid into a gas.

evaporite
A mineral formed after a body of water that contains salts, such as a lake or inland sea, evaporates.

extrusive rock
Igneous rock that forms on Earth's surface from cooled lava, volcanic material, falling ash, or mudflows.

face
A flat surface on a crystal or gemstone. Faces that are cut by humans or machines are called facets.

fault
A line of weakness or a crack in the crust along which a plate of rock can shift or slide. Earthquakes happen when rocks move along faults.

feeder pipe
A tube that brings magma to the opening of a volcano.

fertilizer
A substance spread on soil to restore essential minerals and help crops grow quickly and healthily.

fine grained
Having small grains or crystals.

fluorescent
Having the property of giving off colored light when viewed in ultraviolet light, or glowing in the dark.

focus
The center of an earthquake. Energy spreads out in waves from this point.

forge
A blacksmith's workshop.

fossil
Any trace of an animal or plant from the past, preserved as rock. Fossils may be of bones, shells, flowers, leaves, wood, or footprints.

fossil fuel
A natural fuel, such as coal or gas, formed from the fossil remains of living organisms.

gemstone
A mineral that can be cut, polished, and used in jewelry. Gems are often colorful, rare, and valuable.

geologist
A scientist who specializes in the study of the origin, history, and structure of Earth.

grain
A small particle of rock in a sedimentary rock, or a fleck of mineral in an igneous or metamorphic rock.

habit
The outward appearance of a mineral, as it can be seen with the naked eye. A mineral's particular habit is due to its chemical composition and the conditions in which it grew.

hexagonal
Having a six-sided shape.

hoodoo
A tall, thin spire of rock in arid (dry) terrain. Hoodoos are also known as tent rocks, fairy chimneys, or earth pyramids.

igneous rock
A rock that forms from cooled magma or lava. An igneous rock is composed mainly of interlocking mineral crystals.

impurity
An atom or chemical compound incorporated into the crystal structure of a mineral that is not an essential part of its makeup. Impurities can affect the colors of certain minerals and gemstones.

intrusion
A body of igneous rock that invades an older rock.

intrusive rock
Igneous rock that forms beneath Earth's surface from cooled magma.

laccolith
A large intrusion of igneous rock with a flat base and a dome-shaped top.

lava
Molten rock that erupts at Earth's surface. Lava is called magma when it is still underground.

lodestone
A piece of magnetite or other naturally magnetic mineral or rock.

luster
The way that a mineral reflects light, and what its surface looks like.

magma
Molten rock that can crystallize underground or erupt at Earth's surface as lava.

magma chamber
A large body of molten rock underground. Intruded from deep within Earth, it can feed a volcano with fresh magma or cool slowly to form a batholith or laccolith.

mammal
A warm-blooded animal that gives birth to live young and produces milk to feed them. Mammals live on land and in water; they include elephants, whales, bats, gorillas, and humans.

mantle
The rocky layer lying underneath Earth's crust. Divided into the upper and lower mantles, it contains over 80 percent of Earth's total volume. It is a gooey solid that moves very slowly, driving the motion of tectonic plates.

19.3: the number of times denser than water chengdeite—the densest mineral—is

metamorphic rock
A rock that has been transformed into a new type of rock by heat, pressure, or both.

metamorphism
The process that changes sedimentary and igneous rocks into metamorphic rock.

meteor
A rock from outer space that passes through and burns up in Earth's atmosphere. Meteors are also called shooting stars.

meteorite
A rock from outer space that reaches Earth's surface instead of burning up in the atmosphere.

microscopic
Visible only with the aid of a microscope.

mineral
A naturally occurring, inorganic material with a specific chemical composition and, usually, a crystalline structure.

molten
In a liquid state, due to extreme heat.

native element
A mineral that consists of a single chemical element, not combined with other substances.

nitrate mineral
One of a class of minerals that contain nitrogen bonded tightly to oxygen. Nitrate minerals are evaporites, and many are used as fertilizers.

ooid
A small, spherical grain made of concentric layers of calcite deposited in warm, shallow seawater. Ooids make up oolite rocks.

opaque
Not permitting light to pass through; the opposite of transparent. Opaque substances cannot be seen through.

ore
Any rock that contains minerals from which metal can be extracted.

organism
A living thing; a life-form.

ornate
Having an intricate shape or being decorated with complex patterns.

oxide mineral
One of a class of minerals that are mostly composed of metal atoms bonded tightly to oxygen. Oxide minerals are often associated with igneous rocks.

parent rock
The original rock from which a metamorphic rock was formed.

phosphate mineral
One of a class of minerals that contain phosphorus bonded tightly to oxygen. Phosphate minerals are important in keeping living things healthy.

plate boundary
The line along which two or more tectonic plates meet. Boundaries can be divergent (where plates pull apart and form new crust), convergent (where one plate slides under another and crust is destroyed), or transform (where plates slide past one another).

Crystal shapes
Nailhead spar, with its flat-topped crystals, is an example of one of the more than 300 different shapes that calcite crystals can form.

polyp
An individual member of a coral colony.

pore
A hole, such as a gas bubble in an igneous rock, or a space between grains in a sedimentary rock. Pores can make rocks permeable—water is able to pass through them—or make them capable of storing large quantities of water.

prominent
Important, noticeable, or protruding.

pulsar
A dense neutron star that emits a regular pulse of electromagnetic radiation as it rotates very quickly.

raw material
A basic substance from which a product is made.

reptile
An animal with scaly skin that lay eggs on dry land. Reptiles include lizards, snakes, and crocodiles.

rock
A solid material that forms on or under Earth's surface, made of mineral grains.

salt flat
A flat, dry expanse of ground that is covered with salt and other evaporite minerals. Any pools of water that may form evaporate quickly. The Salar de Uyuni, in Bolivia, is the largest salt flat in the world.

scalpel
A very sharp blade, often used in surgery.

sediment
Particles transported by water or wind, then deposited on the ground or in an underwater bed. In time, these particles may compress into solid rock. Sediments include silt, sand, and the remains of dead plants and animals.

sedimentary rock
A rock that is formed when grains of sediment accumulate, compress, dry out, and solidify.

silica
The common name for the mineral silicon dioxide. Quartz is silica. It is most often found as grains of sand.

silicate mineral
One of a class of minerals that contain silicon and oxygen. Silicate minerals are the most common on Earth, making up about 90 percent of the minerals in the crust. There are many subgroups of silicate minerals.

sill
A horizontal intrusion of magma that hardens to form igneous rock in the cracks of older rocks.

solidify
To turn from a liquid into a solid.

spar
A type of crystal with clearly defined faces.

speleothem
A structure formed in a cave by minerals deposited from water. Stalactites and stalagmites are examples of speleothems.

stalactite
A long, thin deposit of carbonate minerals, hanging from the ceiling of a cave.

stalagmite
A tall, thin deposit of carbonate minerals, rising from the floor of a cave.

Eating clay is called geophagy— some people think it is good for their health

stromatolite
A solid structure composed of the remains of algae that grew in warm, shallow water and then formed microscopically thin layers that built up into football-size mounds over millions of years. Stromatolites are some of the oldest fossils on Earth.

sulfate mineral
One of a class of minerals that contain sulfur bonded tightly to oxygen.

sulfide mineral
One of a class of minerals that are mostly composed of metal atoms bonded tightly to sulfur. Sulfide minerals are often associated with volcanic activity, and many are important metal ores.

tectonic plate
A continent-size slab of Earth's crust. Tectonic plates fit together like a jigsaw puzzle but jostle one another at the boundaries where their edges meet. Neighboring plates crunch together, drift apart, or slide past one another. Earthquakes happen most often at these plate boundaries.

texture
The surface characteristics of something. For a rock, this includes the sizes and shapes of the grains and minerals within it, the relationships between the grains, and their orientation.

transparent
Allowing light to pass through. Something transparent is clear enough that you can see through it.

vein
A thin sheet of minerals that fills a crack or fracture in a rock.

weathering
The breaking down of rocks and minerals into smaller pieces by physical, chemical, and biological processes.

Index